PREVENTING FACE TO FACE VIOLENCE :
Dealing with Anger and Aggression at Work

A Distance Learning Programme

Edition 4

Developed and Written by
William Davies and Neil Frude

Illustrated by
Tim Parker

First published by The Association for Psychological Therapies 1993
Fourth edition published by The APT Press 2000
Reprinted 2001

British Library Cataloguing-in-Publication Data
A catalogue record for this book is available from the British Library

ISBN No. 0 9520914 7 X

Copyright – APT, The Association for Psychological Therapies 1995
PO Box 3, Thurnby, Leicester LE7 9QN

Printed in England by Flexpress, Leicester

CONTENTS

INTRODUCTION

MODULE ONE: THEORY
UNDERSTANDING ANGER, AGGRESSION AND VIOLENCE IN THE WORKPLACE

- Chapter 1:1   *Defining our Terms*

- Chapter 1:2   *A Model for Understanding Aggressive Incidents*

     1:2.1   *- The Situation*

     1:2.2   *- Appraisal*

     1:2.3   *- Anger*

     1:2.4   *- Inhibition*

     1:2.5   *- Aggression*

- Chapter 1:3   *Implications and Application*

- Chapter 1:4   *Risk Assessment*

MODULE TWO: PREVENTION
RISK MANAGEMENT

- Chapter 2.1   *Precautions*

     2:1.1   *- Our Role*

     2:1.2   *- Personal Precautions*

     2:1.3   *- For Those Who Work In Offices*

     2:1.4   *- Special Section – Office Design and Layout*

     2:1.5   *- In Wards and Residential Settings*

     2:1.6   *- When Visiting Someone's Home*

     2:1.7   *- When Escorting People*

     2:1.8   *- In Classrooms*

     2:1.9   *- Organisational Precautions*

     2:1.10   *- Organisational Precautions:* Understanding Resistance

- Chapter 2:2   *Our Attitudes Towards Clients.*

MODULE THREE: INTERACTION
INTERACTING WITH AN AGGRESSIVE CLIENT

- **Part One: Handling Aggressive People**

  Chapter 3:1   *Our Non-Verbal Behaviour*

  Chapter 3:2   *Our Script*

  3:2.1   *- General Verbal Strategies*

  3:2.2   *- Specific Verbal Strategies*

- **Part Two: Admitting Defeat**

  Chapter 3:3   *Escape*

  Chapter 3:4   *What to do if you are Attacked*

  Chapter 3:5   *What to do if a colleague is being Attacked*

MODULE FOUR: POST-INCIDENT
POST-INCIDENT EFFECTS AND INTERVENTIONS

- Chapter 4:1   *Psychological Reactions to Incidents*

- Chapter 4:2   *Support Following an Attack*

  4:2.1   *- Self Help*

  4:2.2   *- Helping a Colleague*

  4:2.3   *- The Manager's Role*

- Chapter 4:3   *Conclusion*

FURTHER READING

INTRODUCTION

A General Comment

When people think of safety at work they normally think of such things as danger from machinery, pollutants, fires and so on. However, for those whose work involves dealing with *people*, a high proportion of the danger comes from interaction with those who are angry, aggressive, or disturbed.

The Legal Background: A Shared Responsibility

The Health and Safety at Work Act (1974) stipulates that it is an employer's duty to ensure, as far as is reasonably practicable, the health, safety and welfare of their employees whilst at work. The same Act also stipulates that all employees have a duty to take reasonable care of their own and other people's health and safety.

The Costs of Violence Against Staff

For the employer, violence against staff may mean a high turnover in staff, lost working days, low commitment, poor service delivery and high insurance costs. In extreme circumstances, it can also mean high financial settlements.

For the employee, violence in the workplace may mean a poor quality of working life, fear and anxiety, loss of commitment and confidence, and difficult relationships with clients and colleagues. Stresses induced in the workplace may also lead to difficulties and friction in the home. And in extreme cases, violence at work may lead to a loss of livelihood through premature retirement or burn-out. In rare cases, it can even mean permanent injury or loss of life.

The Role of Training

By helping to develop safety consciousness, and by providing effective strategies for preventing the build-up of anger in others, training can bring about many valuable effects:

- A reduction in the number of injuries

- A reduction in verbal abuse

- A reduction in the psychological effects of attacks or threats by clients

- An improvement in the response by colleagues and management following such an attack or threats

- A reduction in resentment and dissatisfaction

This last point is important.

> *"Satisfied customers*
> *- or people who realise*
> *we are doing our job fairly -*
> *do not hit us."*

The fact is that many of the techniques which are recommended for avoiding an aggressive response by a client reflect ideal professional practice as it applies in *all* interactions with clients. They help the client to understand the situation realistically, to appreciate what we can and cannot do.

The Limits of Training

However intense a training programme in this area might be, it cannot provide a guaranteed safety shield. No training course can provide a cure-all that eliminates all danger from every situation with every client. BUT, the frequency and intensity of violent incidents may be dramatically reduced by following the principles and strategies included in a good training programme.

The current programme includes a lot of information. Don't feel that you need to learn everything by heart. But having read the information contained in this book, and having worked through the various exercises, alone, or in discussion groups, you will have absorbed very many useful principles. When you have completed the programme, your approach to difficult clients will probably have changed much more than you realize.

Not that we are starting from scratch, however. Any programme such as this can only build on good common sense, much of which will probably have evolved in our professional practice. We are merely trying to top this up by providing insight into the processes by which dangerous incidents occur and some information about well-tried strategies for avoiding or escaping from threatening situations.

THIS TRAINING PROGRAMME IS IN FOUR MODULES CORRESPONDING TO THE T-PIP™ ACRONYM:

Module One
Theory: Understanding Anger, Aggression and Violence in the Workplace

Module Two
Prevention: Assessing Danger and Taking Precautions

Module Three
Interaction: In the Presence of an Aggressive Client

Module Four
Post-Incident: Afterwards

As they are presented in this book, each Module is designed to take roughly two hours. You will be reading for only a part of that time, because the course needs participation in a number of exercises which are introduced throughout the text. These are varied in form, but they are mostly paper-and-pencil exercises. Actually, this under-rates what is involved - mostly they are *thinking* exercises.

When you have completed the total eight-hour programme, you will have thought a great deal about various aspects of the prevention of violence at work and will have read material which represents the distilled experience of hundreds of professionals who have participated in workshops or research projects.

We have tried to keep the exercises brief. We have included them because the programme needs your active involvement. Thinking about a problem ourselves before we read the relevant material adds greatly to the effectiveness of our learning and allows us to think constructively about issues as they apply in our own particular work setting and with our own client group.

One other thing that you can do to make sure that you are studying this book, rather than simply reading it, **is to work through it with a highlighter pen,** marking passages that seem particularly important or particularly relevant to your work situation.

And, finally, a note on terminology. We use the terms *'professional'* and *'client'*. By 'professional' we mean you; by 'client' we mean the people you normally deal with, whether they are schoolchildren, parents, patients in hospital or at home, members of the public, people on probation, customers in a pub or club, or whoever.

We hope that you find the programme informative, enjoyable to complete and useful in your work with clients.

William Davies and Neil Frude

KEY:

     A WRITTEN EXERCISE

     DISCUSSION TOPIC

     PAUSE FOR THOUGHT

MODULE ONE: THEORY

UNDERSTANDING ANGER, AGGRESSION AND VIOLENCE IN THE WORKPLACE

AIMS:

1. **To consider the nature of anger, aggression and violence.**

2. **To provide a model of aggressive incidents and explore relevant aspects of this model in some detail.**

3. **To consider implications of the model for our day to day practice.**

4. **To look at how we can assess the risk involved.**

CHAPTER 1:1

DEFINING OUR TERMS

Let's start straightway with an exercise.

EXERCISE 1:1

 Spend 3 or 4 minutes thinking about the meaning of each of the words: ANGER, AGGRESSION, and VIOLENCE. Jot down some notes about their meanings here:

ANGER

-
-
-
-
-

AGGRESSION

-
-
-
-
-

VIOLENCE

-
-
-
-
-

Now briefly consider the *relationship* between ANGER and AGGRESSION

A: Does ANGER always lead to aggression?   Yes/No   Why?

-
-
-
-
-
-

B: Are people ever AGGRESSIVE when they are NOT angry?   Yes/No Why?

-
-
-
-
-
-

When you've written your notes, turn to the next page where a discussion of relevant points begins. *Don't be tempted to turn over before you have done your bit however!*

DISCUSSION OF EXERCISE 1:1

 The first thing to say is that issues of definition are not right or wrong - different people often have different meanings for the same words. The important thing is what issues this exercise brought to mind. Here are some points which you may have thought about:

ANGER:

- Anger is a feeling or emotion

- It is often a response to something that has happened

- It is often triggered by frustration of some sort

- It may lead to aggression, but doesn't always

- It may be helpful, for example, in getting somebody motivated to tackle a problem

- It is often visible – an angry person may look angry, with Clenched fists etc

AGGRESSION:

- Aggression is an action or behaviour, although it is often associated with an emotion such as anger or frustration

- It is usually intended to hurt someone in some way

- It takes many different forms, verbal or physical, including insults, gestures, slapping, kicking, using weapons

VIOLENCE:

- The term 'violence' is often used when speaking about serious physical attacks

- Like aggression, it may be directed at objects as well as people.

And what did you make of the *RELATIONSHIP* between ANGER and AGGRESSION?

There were two questions:

A: *Does ANGER always lead to aggression?*

It's fairly clear that the answer is NO. The emotional feeling of anger is not always openly expressed as an aggressive action. *The feeling may not be strong enough to motivate the person to become aggressive.* Or, many people bottle up their feelings of anger, although they may explode later.

People are often inhibited for various reasons about expressing their anger as aggression. For example, if our boss makes us angry we may bite our lip because we fear the possible consequences of speaking out. Or, we might well be inhibited about showing our aggression when the person who has made us angry is much stronger than we are, or has a weapon.

In the work context, remember that someone may become angry with us, or our organisation, but inhibit those feelings of anger, and not become aggressive. Sometimes, of course, we will become angry during our work, although our professional position will inhibit us from expressing it.

So, ANGER does *not* always lead to aggression, because either:

- the person is not angry enough, or

- the person inhibits the anger.

Secondly,

B: *Are people ever AGGRESSIVE when they are not angry?*

This is a more tricky question. The answer this time seems to be YES. Think about the example of a bank robber:

- He or she is probably not angry with the cashier; the aggression exhibited is simply *instrumental* in obtaining the money.

Indeed, psychologists make the distinction between two types of aggression:

> - **HOSTILE aggression, which is caused by anger, and**
>
> - **INSTRUMENTAL aggression, which is not driven by anger but by the desire to achieve something. Money, for example, or power.**

Much of the aggression directed at us is hostile aggression - the person is angry. But sometimes their aggression will be instrumental. For example:

- in a residential home, a resident may think that aggression will frighten the professional into giving in on a disciplinary matter.

- a motorist may think that aggression will deter a parking officer from issuing a parking ticket.

- some people may think that aggression will persuade a social worker to give money when there is no entitlement to it.

- a customer may believe that aggression will deter a landlord from evicting him from a pub.

- a parent may think that aggression will persuade a teacher to favour their child at school.

It's worth remembering this important distinction. When someone becomes aggressive or threatening it may be that s/he is not angry but is hoping to gain something from the aggressive behaviour. Nevertheless for the most part, we will be talking about Hostile Aggression in this book, this is the most common.

CHAPTER 1:2

A MODEL FOR UNDERSTANDING AGGRESSIVE INCIDENTS

When considering human aggression it is often useful to have a simple picture, or model, as an aid to understanding. When we are thinking about what leads up to an insult, a fist flying, or another aggressive action, we are focussing on an aggressive incident. This might be something which lasts just a few seconds, or it may be the outcome of something which has been building up for many hours.

For now, let's think about what may **trigger** an aggressive action and the stages that lead from the trigger to the aggressive act itself.

The diagram below presents a simple model of what often happens in an incident that ends in aggressive behaviour. It has five stages.

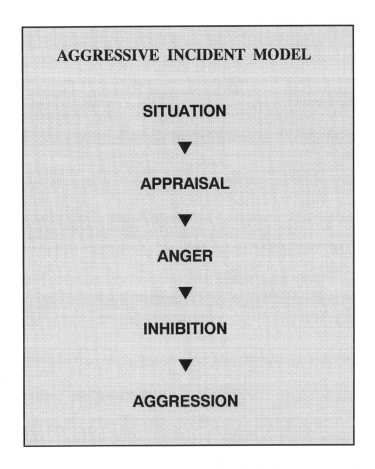

Let's use the model to consider someone having their foot stepped upon.

- The **SITUATION** is the toe being stepped on, causing pain, dirtying the shoe, etc.

- The **APPRAISAL** is the interpretation the person puts on that event. Especially the judgement about whether the person did it deliberately or accidentally.

- The way in which the **situation** is **appraised** affects how much **ANGER** is experienced. This is so, even though some people are more easily roused to anger than others; they have a short fuse.

- Anger is often **INHIBITED** by fear of retaliation, for example, or anxiety about injuring the other person. So not all anger becomes aggression.

- Finally, when **AGGRESSION** does occur it can take any one of many different forms, from a murmured insult at one extreme to a wild physical attack at the other.

Here's another example :

- We ask someone to do something - SITUATION

- This is regarded by the person as unfair - APPRAISAL

- The person becomes - ANGRY

- The person lacks self-control i.e. his/her INHIBITIONS are weak

- AGGRESSION occurs

This model illustrates how there are many points at which aggression can be prevented. Using the last example, aggression may have been prevented by, for example:

- The professional not asking the person (avoiding the SITUATION)

- The person viewing the request as fair (APPRAISAL)

- The person being able to recognize and control his/her ANGER

- The person being INHIBITED by the fear of possible consequences of aggression

So, breaking the chain at any point along the Model from beginning to end could be sufficient to prevent dangerous aggression.

The next series of exercises has been designed to highlight important features of the Aggressive Incident Model.

The first concerns the initial triggers to anger, the SITUATIONS that may lead someone to act in an aggressive manner.

CHAPTER 1:2.1

SITUATION
·
APPRAISAL
·
ANGER
·
INHIBITION
·
AGGRESSION

EXERCISE 1:2   ANGER TRIGGERS

 Suggest various ways of making someone angry. Try to make the list as diverse as possible. If we need inspiration it often helps to imagine how we might make our partner angry! Then move on to consider how you can make people angry at work, and in social situations.

At home or with close relations:

-
-
-

At work:

-
-
-

Socially:

-
-
-

DISCUSSION OF EXERCISE 1:2

Some of the points that may have cropped up as you completed the exercise are:

- There are many different ways of making people angry.

- Different people get angry about different things. People have special sensitivities eg. "He hates it when I fiddle with my hair", "She can't stand it when I try to imitate her Scottish accent".

- We have a lot of knowledge about how to make other people angry. And so do others, including those we meet in the course of our work.

Certain basic elements appear in many of the situations that people suggest. One analysis suggests that there are basically three ELEMENTS that lead to anger:

1) IRRITANTS - such as loud noises, bad smells

2) COSTS - things that involve some personal loss including losses of money, goods, 'face' or status

3) TRANSGRESSIONS - a person breaking a rule or doing something that is out of order

Every situation that makes people angry appears to have at least one of these elements. Some have two of the elements, and some have all three.

For example, someone smoking in a non-smoking carriage of a train is likely to trigger the anger of fellow passengers. Why?

- There may be an IRRITANT factor. Smoke causing bad air and smells.

- There may be a COST factor. People may feel that their health is being put in danger.

- And there is clearly a TRANSGRESSION factor. Smoking in a non-smoking carriage is against the rules.

CHAPTER 1:2.2

SITUATION

.

<u>APPRAISAL</u>

.

ANGER

.

INHIBITION

.

AGGRESSION

Situations often trigger anger. But it is not the situations in themselves that produce the emotional response. It is not someone stepping on my toe that makes me angry, *but how I judge that action* - my **appraisal** in other words (in this case, whether I think the person trod on my foot accidentally or deliberately). *Many situations can be interpreted in a number of ways, and the precise interpretation will determine the emotional impact.*

The appraisal someone makes of a situation depends on many things, including:

- **The way they generally view things**

- **The person's mood at the time. People who are already angry tend to view things in a negative way**

- **What other people are saying about the situation**

Most social situations can be appraised in very different ways, some of which will lead to anger and some of which will not. For example, suppose I pass a friend or acquaintance and s/he doesn't acknowledge me. I might say to myself:

- *"S/he was deliberately ignoring me."*

- *"S/he simply didn't see me."*

- *"S/he might have been anxious about something and was probably preoccupied."*

- *"S/he was acting in a superior way - being snobbish."*

If I interpret the situation along the lines suggested by either the first or last, I might well become angry. On the other hand, the two other responses are more charitable and well-disposed towards the other person and would be unlikely to result in anger.

Appraisal differences have been shown to be important in explaining many different types of aggression. In the case of marital violence, a man who is watching his partner put on make-up before an evening out together, might think:

- *"She wants to look attractive"* or

- *"She wants to make herself attractive for me"* or

- *"She is trying to make herself attractive to other men"*

The last of these would usually be most likely to lead to anger.

Appraisal analysis is also important in understanding physical child abuse. Suppose a baby is crying. Which of the following appraisals would be likely to lead to ANGER?:

1. *"He is teething."*   YES/NO

2. *"She is crying deliberately to disturb me."*   YES / NO

3. *"She is exercising her lungs like all babies do."*   YES / NO

Here it is the second example that may very well lead directly to anger.

Let's orientate ourselves. Where are we in this Module!?

We are working our way through the **Aggressive Incident Model.** Here it is again:

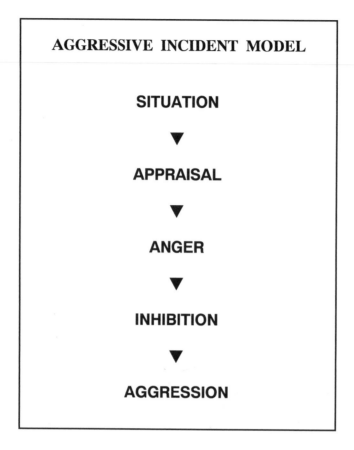

We have so far examined the **SITUATION** stage - considering the kinds of situations and events that act as triggers to anger - and we then moved on to consider **APPRAISAL**.

Next is **ANGER ...**

CHAPTER 1:2.3

The third stage of the Model is:

SITUATION

·

APPRAISAL

·

ANGER

·

INHIBITION

·

AGGRESSION

Having already considered the concept of anger in exercise 1, we know that anger is an EMOTIONAL STATE which *SOMETIMES* leads to aggression.

We can now examine the nature of this emotional state in a little more detail. As well as the feeling of anger, the emotional state is accompanied by:

- *biological changes,* **eg. heart-thumping, tense muscles, fast breathing, raised blood pressure.**

- *behavioural changes,* **eg. fast and loud speech, movements that tell us the person is on edge, and stereotyped movements such as drumming fingers on a table, or rocking.**

It is the behavioural signs that often tell us that someone is angry and we should therefore recognize them as risk signs.

THE DYNAMICS OF ANGER

Many theories of human aggression use the metaphor of anger as a fluid. As anger is generated by different events it builds up, like the level of water in a bucket as more water is poured into it. At a certain point it may overflow. As water is taken out of the bucket, the level subsides. The idea, then, is that anger builds up unless it is discharged in some way. It may also simply seep away in time without being discharged in an aggressive action. This is a useful way of looking at anger, and it corresponds with most people's observations of their own and other people's anger. Let's consider the dynamics of anger in terms of three phenomena:

1) ANGER CAN *ACCUMULATE*:

Most of us have been in a situation, say in a pub or restaurant, where a faulty door fails to close automatically and it is irritating when someone comes in and leaves the door open. Imagine sitting there while a whole succession of people walk through at 30-second intervals. After the first person has left the door open we would probably get up and shut it. When the second person leaves it open we might become a little irritated. After the third person, the fourth person and the fifth person have come through the door, we would probably be very angry, and possibly openly aggressive. This even though their action was *precisely* the same as the first person who left the door open. What has happened, of course, is that our own anger level has gradually increased, or accumulated.

When an individual's anger has built up to an extreme pitch, another person may come with the straw that breaks the camel's back. Although that person's action has been only slightly provocative in itself, s/he may feel the full force of the individual's pent-up anger. This explains why people's aggressive response sometimes seems totally disproportionate to the event which apparently triggered it.

2) ANGER CAN BE DISPLACED:

This simply refers to the fact that anger generated by one person may be displaced to someone else.

- *Anger generated by someone in a Council Housing department, for example, may be the source of aggression directed towards someone in the Social Services department.*

- *Anger generated by a peer in a residential setting may be taken out on one of the people providing care.*

So when we become the target of verbal abuse we may ask ourselves: *"What did I do?"* Sometimes the answer will be *"very little"*, the truth being that anger generated in another context has been directed at us simply because we were there.

3) CATHARSIS:

Finally, a phenomenon that has attracted much discussion and research, but which remains highly controversial, is that of catharsis. The idea is that if an angry person acts aggressively, or blows off steam in some way, they may have discharged some of their anger so that it returns to a safe level.

Relatively safe and acceptable ways of blowing off steam include: screaming or thumping a pillow repeatedly. Other ways, which are not to be recommended, include throwing darts at a picture of the aggression target, and driving at top speed down a motorway. There are of course many ways of reducing anger which do not involve catharsis, including relaxing, taking a warm bath, listening to soothing music and the like.

If we are faced with someone who admits to his or her anger, and is in effect asking for a non-aggressive way out, we might suggest one of the safer cathartic methods or, preferably, one of the soothing techniques. However, in most confrontations the person is not asking for help in remaining calm, and any suggestion that they might benefit from chopping wood or taking a bath would merely add fuel to the fire.

The next exercise asks you to draw upon your own experience (either as a professional or in other areas of your life) to come up with some illustrative examples of the three kinds of anger dynamics discussed in this section.

EXERCISE 1:3
MY EXPERIENCE OF ANGER DYNAMICS

 Think about the phenomena of accumulation, displacement and catharsis and try to remember examples of each of these as they have occurred in your own experience. Either in your professional or your personal life. Use the spaces below to jot down a few notes on each topic.

ACCUMULATION:

-
-
-
-

DISPLACEMENT:

-
-
-
-

CATHARSIS:

-
-
-
-

This exercise is an important one, entirely for your own benefit. No DISCUSSION follows.

CHAPTER 1:2.4

The fourth stage of the Model is:

SITUATION

·

APPRAISAL

·

ANGER

·

INHIBITION

·

AGGRESSION

It is clear that anger is not always openly expressed. Indeed, even when someone is extremely angry they may not show it. Why is this? The answer is that people are often inhibited about expressing their anger. This might not necessarily be a good thing - there is some evidence to suggest that those who are chronically unable to express their anger may develop high blood pressure for example, as a consequence.

In the context we are considering, we certainly hope that people make their grievances and frustrations known, but we also hope that they will inhibit any extreme aggression.

In some cases aggression is inhibited physically by someone else. For example, the person may be held using a particular control and restraint tactic. But most inhibitions are psychological and reflect particular beliefs and judgements that help the person to hold back his or her aggression. Some inhibitions, sometimes labelled *external inhibitions* reflect the external situation. For example, the person may judge that the other person is far stronger than s/he is. Other inhibitions, labelled *internal inhibitions* reflect personal beliefs, including *"I'm a pacifist - I don't believe in being physically aggressive"* and *"If I hurt this person I would never be able to forgive myself"*.

The next exercise concerns inhibitors of both these types.

EXERCISE 1:4
INTERNAL AND EXTERNAL INHIBITORS

 Spend a few minutes thinking about internal and external inhibitors - perceptions and ideas that might hold a person back from being aggressive. Write notes in the spaces below:

INTERNAL INHIBITORS:

- eg. strong self-control

-

-

-

EXTERNAL INHIBITORS:

- eg. Fear of physical retaliation

-

-

-

DISCUSSION OF EXERCISE 1:4

Your lists of inhibitors might have included some of the following:

INTERNAL INHIBITORS -

- *strong self-control*

- *anticipated feelings of guilt*

- *moral inhibitions*

EXTERNAL INHIBITORS -

- *fear of physical retaliation*

- *fear of social consequences*

- *fear of legal consequences*

- *fear of material losses*

- *fear of embarrassment*

An element that is common to many of these inhibition factors is that the person holds back because the cost of being aggressive will be too high. However angry someone is, when they are faced with the boss or with someone holding a gun, they do tend to behave in a restrained way.

How does this analysis apply to our work? If the would-be aggressor believes that we have the power to help them, and if they respect our profession, they may well be inhibited about insulting us or being physically aggressive towards us. If, on the other hand, they see our profession as having low status and little power to help them - or even working against them - they may have few inhibitions against being aggressive.

Before we leave the topic of inhibition, two further points are worth noting:

- *If inhibitions are high with respect to one potential target, eg. the boss, but somewhat lower towards another, eg. one's partner, it is likely that displacement will occur.*

- *Inhibitions are relative to particular forms of aggression. For example, I may not feel inhibited about shouting at my child when angry with him, whereas I would feel inhibited about hitting him.*

CHAPTER 1:2.5

Lastly:

SITUATION

·

APPRAISAL

·

ANGER

·

INHIBITION

·

AGGRESSION

We have now come to the final stage of the model. The term aggression clearly covers a very wide range of behaviours - including verbal aggression (insults, jibes, etc.) and physical aggression. Physical aggression includes such vastly different behaviours as slaps, punches, kicks, hitting with a weapon, and shooting. The *FORM* of aggression is very important - indeed it could be a matter of life and death. Earlier we suggested that the dimension of low aggression to high aggression could be thought of as a continuum from a murmur at one end to murder at the other. What factors, then, determine whether the response will be one of murmur or murder?

We'll start by placing the ball in your court, with an exercise designed to examine factors which affect the form of aggression used.

EXERCISE 1:5   FORMS OF AGGRESSION

Think about two men, Con and Dan, in two different pubs. Both became very aggressive when insulted by another man, Vic, but whereas Con reacted in a Con-trolled way by merely shouting at his Vic-tim, Dan reacted in a very Dan-gerous way by smashing a glass and pushing it in the Vic-tim's face ('bottling'). Suggest various explanations for the difference in Con's controlled action and Dan's dangerous action:

·

·

·

DISCUSSION OF EXERCISE 1:5

 A number of important factors are commonly identified as shaping the form of aggression used, and some of these are discussed below. Obviously, no list is definitive, and you should feel that you have done well if you have listed at least some of these factors. You may also have identified others which are not on the list.

1. ANGER LEVEL: Perhaps the most obvious factor. We would expect extreme forms of aggression to be more likely to result from extreme anger. Dan may have 'bottled' Vic because he was extremely angry.

2. INHIBITIONS: If inhibitions do not prevent aggression altogether then they may at least reduce the degree of aggression shown. Con may have been more inhibited about being aggressive than Dan was.

3. PERSONAL BELIEFS: Personal rules can be powerful internal inhibitors of particular forms of aggression. Con and Dan may differ in their personal rules about what is justified and acceptable.

4. HABITS and TRAINING: When they are extremely angry, people tend to use their own habitual form of aggression. Some people scratch, others kick, others use insults. Dan may have broken glasses in pub fights before.

5. OPPORTUNITY: When they are extremely aggressive, people will use whatever is to hand. Dan may have used a glass simply because it was close to hand.

6. PREVIOUS VERBAL THREATS: People often do what they SAY they're going to do. Maybe Dan had already threatened *"Say that again and you'll get a glass in your face."*

7. RECIPROCITY: Those who are bitten tend to bite back; those who are slapped tend to slap back. If Dan had seen Vic reaching for a glass he might have tried simply to get in first.

The following factors are probably not of central importance in the context of work-based aggression (and not really applicable to our Con and Dan story) but we mention them briefly for the sake of completeness.

8) INSTRUMENTAL EFFECTS: Some aggressive actions are designed not only to hurt the victim but also to get something from them, or to bring about a certain response. A screaming child may have a pillow pushed over their face. This is partly 'just' an act of aggression but it also serves to stop the noise of the screaming.

9) VULNERABILITY: Knowing a person's weak spot, the aggressor may deliberately aim for it. A violent husband, in an attack on his wife, for example, may cut off her hair if this is a feature she is most proud of. Insults, especially, are often aimed at the person's most sensitive area.

10) SYMBOLISM & RITUAL: Some aggressive actions have a ritual or symbolic meaning - classic examples include 'tarring and feathering'. In a case a few years ago, an enraged person gave a powerful and symbolic message to his professional helper by ordering an undertaker to turn up at the professional's home.

In summary, many different factors shape the aggressive response, and a knowledge of people's habits, inhibitions and beliefs may help us to predict the particular form their aggression may take.

CHAPTER 1:3

IMPLICATIONS
AND APPLICATION

IMPLICATIONS AND APPLICATION

- There is normally a **situation** that triggers any incident.

  - This means we do well to know just what those situations are in our own job, and do our level best to eliminate - or at least minimise them.

- People **appraise** the same situation in many different ways.

  - If the appraisal is favourable then anger will rarely follow. Therefore, if somebody has 'got hold of the wrong end of the stick', and is agitated about it, we do our best to set the record straight.

- A third point of possible intervention is at the **anger** stage.

  - Anger can both accumulate and be displaced. If we're the victim, phrases like *'Look, it's just that this is the last straw for you'* or *'Look, it's not really me you're angry with, is it?'*, can <u>sometimes</u> be very powerful.

- Even if the situation, the appraisal and the level of anger remain unchanged, it may still be possible to prevent aggression by increasing **inhibitions**.

  - A social worker who warns a parent: *"If another bruise appears on the child, there is every chance that the child will have to be taken into care"*, is increasing the external factors that might inhibit the parent from hitting the child.

- Even at the final stage - where **aggression** is exhibited - we can still influence the form it takes

  - by for example limiting the availability of potential weapons (eg heavy ashtrays, letter-openers, etc).

CHAPTER 1:4

RISK ASSESSMENT

Having established a theoretical model, we can use it to predict the risk of aggressive incidents. Clearly, not everyone is equally vulnerable to attack by the people they deal with. Some professions are more at risk than others.

For example, within the nursing profession, those who work in Accident and Emergency departments are more at risk that those who work in children's wards. And the risk in Accident and Emergency is highest late on Friday and Saturday nights.

The next exercise asks you to select, from groups of three professionals, which one you think might be most at risk of attack by the people they work with. Its purpose is to help us to think about the various elements or factors that contribute to a professional's risk of attack.

EXERCISE 1:6   WHICH JOB IS MOST VULNERABLE?

This exercise asks you to think about each of three different sets of professions. For each set, decide which of the three professionals you think might be most at risk of being injured by someone in the course of their work. Enter 'A' or 'B' or 'C' beside the group. Then, (and this is the important part of the exercise) provide one or two reasons WHY you think this professional might be at more risk than the other two.

A: G.P.s   B: Psychiatrists   C: Teachers   .....

WHY?

*

*

A: Police   B: Probation Officers   C: Nurses   .....

WHY?

- •

- •

A: Ambulance personnel   **B: Social workers**
          C: Residential workers with adolescents   .....

WHY?

- •

- •

DISCUSSION OF EXERCISE 1:6

Once again, we are not concerned with right answers. In many cases a perfectly good case could be made out for any of the three professionals in a set being the most at risk. The purpose of the exercise was to help uncover some of the key factors that might add to the risk of *any* profession, including our own.

Let's take a look at the first trio.

A: G.P.s   B: Psychiatrists   C: Teachers

In workshops, we find that most people opt for either psychiatrists or teachers and here are some of the reasons given to support a choice of each of the three:

G.P.s:

Factors that INCREASE risk:

- • They visit people in their own home.

- • May visit mentally disturbed people in an acute state.

- • May give alarming medical news.

- • May be held responsible for mistakes, by other family members.

- • May carry drugs which the assailant wants.

Factors that DECREASE risk:

- They are usually held in high regard.

- Seen as helping and being on the patient's side.

PSYCHIATRISTS:

Factors that INCREASE risk:

- Deal with highly disturbed people.

- Patients may be deluded.

- Patients may be held against their will.

Factors that DECREASE risk:

- Usually held in high regard, Consultant status might help.

- Seen as helping and being on the patient's side.

TEACHERS:

Factors that INCREASE risk:

- Large number of pupils dealt with simultaneously.

- Prolonged contact may lead to the development of deep antagonisms.

- Have disciplinary role.

- May be dealing with pupils who do not want to be in school and regard teachers as enemies rather than friends or helpers.

- May have low status in the eyes of some pupils and parents.

Factors that DECREASE risk:

- May be dealing with younger (less threatening) pupils.

Let's look at just three other professions and their associated risks:

POLICE:

- Are often called to situations that are already violent.

- Have a major disciplinary role.

- Are members of a profession that some people are antagonistic to.

- Often carry out risky tasks, e.g. making an arrest.

SOCIAL WORKERS:

- Deal with people under stress.

- Are often unable to supply what the client needs e.g. money, good accommodation, employment.

- May be involved in extremely provocative situations such as taking a child into care.

- Have low status in the eyes of some people.

PUBLICANS:

- Deal with people who may be intoxicated.

- May have to refuse a request. For example, for another drink after closing time.

- Required to get some people to do what they don't want to, e.g. leave the pub.

- May have to intervene in arguments between customers.

SOME THEMES NOW EMERGING:

It is clear that some **people** are higher-risk than others. A person who is habitually threatening, for example, can be considered higher-risk than someone who rarely becomes angry and who shows respect for professionals.

Some **tasks** are clearly more risky than others. For example a police officer might be at relatively high risk when arresting someone who is very drunk.

It is also the case that some **settings** are more risky than others. For example, a setting in which we are confined with someone in a relatively small room, with only one exit, with no panic alarm, and out of earshot of colleagues, is clearly more risky than a setting in which we are in full public view.

EXERCISE 1:7   ASSESSING THE RISK

We have suggested that:

- *some people are higher-risk than others*

- *some tasks are more risky than others*

- *some settings are more risky than others*

Our task is to think about all these factors.

One way of tackling this exercise is to think in terms of a Risk Assessment Inventory. That is, a checklist which includes a large number of danger signs or danger factors. Typically, a Risk Assessment inventory reflects relevant characteristics of the <u>person,</u> the <u>task</u> and the <u>setting</u>, and the number of ticks is then added to provide an overall measure of risk.

So, one way of going about this exercise would be to imagine that you have been asked to produce the first draft of a risk-assessment inventory. What items would you include on the checklist? *Use the headings provided below, and write down, for each, a number of factors that you judge to be linked to increased risk.*

PERSON

- (eg.) has a history of violence

-

-

TASK

- (eg.) refusing something

-

-

SETTING

- (eg.) small room, one exit

-

-

DISCUSSION OF EXERCISE 1:7

Let's discuss possible answers separately under the three headings, although it should be recognized that many answers could be equally well placed under, say, the 'Person' heading or the 'Task' heading. (For example, 'Refusing something to someone who is drunk' could be seen as a Person factor or as a Task factor.)

1) THE PERSON

You may have included some or all of the following:

- **A Previous Record Of Threats, Anger, Aggression**

    - Has the person been aggressive, or threatened violence, in the past? Any record of such behaviour should make us wary. If the person has a history of having been aggressive towards professionals (perhaps even to our own colleagues, or to us ourselves) then this should increase our estimation of risk considerably.

    - *Implication: Colleagues need to share such information, not just verbally but by writing it down. It is important to include on individuals' written records a general description of any history of aggression and full details about any incident, of either aggression or threat, involving professionals.*

- **Physical Characteristics**

    - Is the person physically strong? If s/he is then s/he may present more risk.

    - Other physical characteristics that would lead some people to judge increased risk include aggressive dress or appearance - certain hairstyles and clothes may identify the person as following an aggressive cult or subculture. Punk was an early example.

    - *Drawback: We may be led into stereotyping errors. Naturally we should guard against automatically feeling fear when we meet someone whose appearance strikes us as odd.*

- **Attitudes And Expectations**

    - The person's attitudes towards our agency, professionals in general, our profession, and us in particular, are closely associated with the level of risk. Those people who feel positively about our agency or our profession will be less likely to become angry with us, and if they are angry with us they will be inhibited about being openly aggressive.

On the other hand, if somebody has negative feelings about us or our agency, or professionals in general, then s/he is much more likely to become angry and aggressive.

- There are several ways in which someone may be hostile. Some see all members of a particular professional as ineffective, overpaid upstarts who know little of what goes on in real life. Other people have a general disdain of anyone in authority. Sometimes the antagonism is restricted to particular sub-classes of people, perhaps those who are young, or old, or female, or male, or those who are members of particular ethnic groups.

- Many people have totally unrealistic expectations of us. They imagine that if we wished to do so, we could move mountains on their behalf. This too is a danger sign, because any failure to come up with the goods is taken as a sign of lack of sympathy, interest or motivation on the part of the professional. *"It's not that you can't"*, such people seem to imply, *"but that you won't"*.

- *Implication:* Any knowledge that an individual has negative opinions about us or unrealistic expectations of what we can achieve, increases our rating of their risk.

- **Temporary aspects of the person**

  - *Is the person currently agitated or in a bad mood?*

  - *Is the person drunk or under the influence of drugs?*

  - *Is the person currently in an acute psychiatric condition?*

  - *Is the person likely to be carrying a weapon?*

  - *Has the person come with a complaint or grudge?*

  - *Is the person abusive or threatening?*

  - *Is the person feeling 'trapped'?*

  - *Have other people been winding him/her up?*

2) THE TASK

There are 2 important headings here:

- **Having to Give Bad News, eg:**

  - saying that we are leaving our current post, or

  - that an application for housing, custody of a child, parole, home help, or

- financial benefit, has been turned down, or

- telling someone they're under arrest, or

- telling a parent their child is unable to do a particular thing.

What might it be in your job?

- **Refusing a person something they want**

  - This is frequently money, or has financial implications, or a particular choice of food (in residential settings), or can be quite specific like not allowing someone on a particular trip they want.

What might it be in your job?

---

3) THE ENVIRONMENT / SETTING

- A 'YES' answer to any one of the following should increase our estimate of risk (and the more 'YES's the more our estimate of risk should rise).

  - *Are you alone with the person?*

  - *Are your colleagues unaware of the fact that you may be in a particularly threatening situation?*

  - *Are you out of your normal workplace?*

  - *Are there potential weapons around?*

- A 'YES' to any of the following will *reduce* the risk estimate.

  - *Is there a telephone or an alarm system?*

  - *Are there obvious escape routes?*

  - *Do you have a plan of what to do if attacked?*

PAUSE FOR THOUGHT

Spend a few minutes thinking about your own work. Think
about the factors identified in the above list and any others
which might contribute to danger for you and your
colleagues.

*This exercise is an important one, and entirely for your own benefit - no
DISCUSSION follows*

PEOPLE:

TASKS:

SETTINGS:

A Risk Assessment Inventory. The more questions that can be answered 'YES' the more risky should we judge the situation to be.

1) THE PERSON

- **Relatively permanent aspects**
  - Has the person a previous record of threats, anger, aggression?
  - Does the person's physical appearance indicate membership of an intentionally aggressive sub-group?
  - Does the person have negative attitudes to our profession?
  - Has he or she got unrealistic expectations?
- **Temporary aspects of the person**
  - Are they currently agitated or in a bad mood?
  - Are they drunk or under the influence of drugs?
  - Are they currently in an acute psychiatric condition?
  - Are they likely to be carrying a weapon?
  - Have they come with a complaint or grudge?
  - Are they abusive or threatening?
  - Are they feeling 'trapped'?
  - Have other people been winding him/her up?

2) THE TASK

- Are we having to give bad news
- Are we refusing to give something the person wants
- Is there a mis-match between what is expected and what we can provide?

3) THE ENVIRONMENT / SETTING

- Are we alone with the person?
- Are our colleagues unaware of the fact that we may be in a particularly threatening situation?
- Are we out of our normal workplace?
- Are there potential weapons around?

A 'YES' to any of the following will *reduce* the risk estimate.

- Is there a telephone or an alarm system?
- Are there obvious escape routes?
- Do we have a plan of what to do if attacked?

CONCLUSION TO MODULE ONE

We have now come to the end of the first Module. You should now feel that you understand the nature of human aggression a little better than you did before embarking on this Module. You may also be beginning to see how

the theoretical analysis of aggression relates to strategies that can be used to by us to interact with people in such a way that the danger of risk or attack is minimized.

UNDERSTANDING *WHY* SOMEBODY IS THREATENING AGGRESSION, AND WHEN WE MIGHT PREDICT AGGRESSION OCCURRING CAN OFTEN HELP TO GENERATE SAFETY STRATEGIES.

In Module Two we will be discussing a range of precautions that can be taken to reduce risk in the workplace.

NOTES

NOTES

MODULE TWO: PREVENTION

RISK MANAGEMENT

AIMS:

1. To consider *precautions* we can take to reduce risk in a range of settings.

2. To consider precautions that can be taken *by an organisation* to help reduce risk.

3. To consider *staff attitudes* that may increase risk, and, conversely, those that will reduce it.

INTRODUCTION

Having spent some time attempting to understand the nature of anger and aggression, Modules Two and Three are principally concerned with strategies that can be used to reduce the risk of threats, attacks and injury.

- The bulk of this Module (Two) considers precautions that we can take, *even before we see the person*, to reduce the risks of attack and injury. These include precautions which we can take ourselves and precautions which may be taken by the organisation.

- The Module ends with a recognition that certain of our attitudes may increase the risk of a situation.

- In Module Three we will be describing ways in which we can tailor our *interaction* with people in order to help maintain our safety.

What happens when we judge that a meeting with a particular person may prove risky? The obvious answer is that we should attempt to take adequate precautions and behave in ways which reduce the risk of threat, attack and injury.

Most of this Module concerns Precautions that can be taken

- *by us individually,*

- *by us together with colleagues,*

- *by managers and policy-makers.*

Much of this training programme concerns risk reduction, and it is not difficult to see how the effectiveness of our attempts to reduce risk will greatly depend on an appropriate *estimate* of the level of risk. The material introduced in Module One therefore provides a good basis. Having recognized elements that increase the level of risk, our task is to consider how such elements may be reduced in their impact, or eliminated.

CHAPTER 2:1

PRECAUTIONS

Precautions are things that can be done before meeting someone, in order to reduce the risk of attack and injury.

There are many things that we can do, and many things that our organisation can do, to reduce the risk of attack or injury. They range from *personal precautions,* such as carrying a personal alarm, to *organisational precautions* such as insisting on a 'checking in' system after home visits. *Our discussion of precautions is divided into a number of sections, not all of which will be equally applicable to you.*

The first two sections below *do* **apply generally, and so does the last one, so put a tick in those three boxes, below, now. Then read through the others on the list, and tick the ones that might** *ever* **apply to you.**

PRECAUTIONS - YOUR ROLE   (tick)

PERSONAL PRECAUTIONS   (tick)

PRECAUTIONS FOR THOSE WHO WORK IN OFFICES

PRECAUTIONS IN WARDS AND RESIDENTIAL HOMES

PRECAUTIONS WHEN VISITING THE CLIENT'S HOME

PRECAUTIONS WHEN ESCORTING CLIENTS

PRECAUTIONS IN CLASSROOMS

ORGANISATIONAL PRECAUTIONS (tick)

As you work through this Module, you will meet these sections in the order given. **Those sections which you have ticked should be studied carefully,** but even if you have not ticked a section you should still quickly read it through because:

- *you might find that it does contain material which, with just slight alteration, you can apply to your work.*

- *your job might change in the future.*

- *the information might help you to advise others.*

CHAPTER 2:1.1

PRECAUTIONS - YOUR ROLE

A great many things can be done before we are actually with the client to reduce the risk of threat, attack or injury. These are precautions that can be addressed in the cold light of day rather than in the heat of the moment.

Precautionary measures arise in many different ways, and from initiatives taken at many different levels. For example:

- *Precautions may be taken as a result of developments in policy.*

- *Precautions may be taken as a result of discussions between you and your colleagues, resulting in special arrangements or agreements.*

- *Precautions may be taken by you as you move into a new office.*

- *Precautions may be taken by you as you are getting ready to go to work for the day.*

- *Precautions may be used by you as you prepare yourself to meet your next client.*

> **Have your working conditions changed recently to increase safety?**
>
> **What (or who) stimulated these changes?**

Some precautions are personal precautions that we can take ourselves, whereas others involve teams working together, and some involve organisational policy and the working conditions provided by the service.

We should be involved in developments at <u>all</u> of these levels. We should of course take whatever personal precautions we feel to be necessary, but we should also participate in, and if necessary stimulate, precautionary developments at the team level. And if we feel that policies or provisions could be changed to increase safety for us and our colleagues then we should let the powers that be know about this, through the appropriate channels.

Many agencies are reactive rather than proactive with respect to safety precautions. Unless they get information and requests from the grass-roots they may assume that the safety of the workforce is adequately provided for. If we and our colleagues recognize that the provision of a panic button in an isolated office would add to safety, for example, or that changing the layout in a reception area would make it safer, then we should discuss the matter with our line manager and make sure that the appropriate authorities are aware of our concerns. We may be pleasantly surprised at how seriously these matters are taken and how swiftly our suggestions are acted upon.

In terms of precautions, our personal responsibility for our own safety extends beyond those things over which we have immediate control. There are, however, many things which we can do entirely on our own initiative, without the need to involve others. Such matters include such issues as how we dress and how we prepare ourselves to see a new client.

The next section concerns such personal precautions.

CHAPTER 2:1.2

PERSONAL PRECAUTIONS

When we talk about Personal Precautions, we mean precautions we might take *wherever we work.* By Precautions we mean things we do *before the client is actually with us.* Specifically:

1. CLOTHES MANAGEMENT

- Avoid provocative clothing. This means not only clothing which may be

    - *sexually provocative,* but also clothing which is

    - *too exclusive,* or, on the other hand,

    - *too downmarket.*

Wearing expensive designer clothing or exclusive jewellery when we may be working with people who are struggling to survive under conditions of poverty, is inappropriate and may alienate and anger our clients. At the other extreme, we want to show respect for our clients and therefore probably wouldn't wear greasy tattered jeans, for example. Obviously, we have rights as well as the client, and we cannot be expected to dress entirely to please clients, but we should avoid extremes.

- Give some thought to t-shirt slogans, badges of political affiliation etc. This is an issue over which people disagree, but we should consider whether a particular badge or slogan might alienate a proportion of our client population.

- Some clothing is potentially risky and could be used as a weapon against us. For this reason, men who deal with high-risk client populations (prison officers and psychiatric nurses, for example), generally wear clip-on ties to avoid the possibility of strangulation.

    - Wearing our hair long can also be risky. If we have very long hair the client may be tempted to pull it or may even attempt to strangle us with it. One option is to simply wear it 'up'.

    - Earrings can also be risky. Those with pierced ears should avoid wearing earrings, or wear clip-ons, or should at least make sure that there is no risk that the ear lobe could be damaged if the earring were to be pulled. Screw-type fastenings with relatively heavy bars passing through the ear-lobe should *never* be worn when dealing with clients. A heavy pull on such an earring can cause a very nasty injury.

2. INFORMATION AWARENESS

- When we are about to see someone for the first time find out as much about him/her as possible. Obviously, we'll need to be informed about their situation in order to help them. Understandably, many clients hate having to repeat information to several different peoples. An enquiry about their circumstances might well meet with an exasperated *"Well I told the other person all about that last week"*.

    - Clients will be impressed and reassured if we appear to know about their circumstances and may be highly dismissive if we get things wrong. In one workshop it emerged that an Educational Welfare Officer who had taken a telephone referral turned up at a house and asked, politely, why the young girl had not been attending school. This was met with anger and derision. The EWO had been asked to call on, as she judged it, the parents of a girl called Lesley Brown. In fact the couple had a son, Leslie. Mistakes like this may be very difficult to avoid, but this story illustrates the point that clients expect us to be informed about their case.

- The client's record may include a note of previous threats or aggression. Being forewarned in this way may raise our risk estimate and may allow us to make appropriate adjustments in terms of where we see the client, what we tell colleagues, etc.

- We may feel, on the basis of the information we have read or have been told about a particular client, that we are not the most appropriate person to deal with him/her.

    - Someone who has previously presented problems to professionals of a certain race, for example, may be better dealt with by somebody else. Clearly, this is a sensitive issue. We don't wish to be seen as ducking responsibility in any way, or as off-loading difficult clients, but we should discuss the matter with colleagues if we feel that we are not the most appropriate person to deal with the client.

3. WORKLOAD MANAGEMENT

- Everybody who works for an organisation of any type has constraints upon them. We are expected to accomplish certain tasks and have, typically, little time in which to do so. But within the constraints imposed upon us, we probably have some degree of freedom about the order in which we do things, the time which can be used to up-date records or write reports, etc.
    - *Don't overload yourself by trying to deal with too many people in a short space of time* or, if the number of people we have to see is fixed,

    - *Don't try to spend too much time with each.* If we have a half an hour set aside for a particular client, we try to complete our interaction with the client well within that time. If we know that the process of finishing a session with an individual always takes a long time, we need to allow for this and begin wrapping up the session ten minutes before the end of the allotted time.

> "*Working behind schedule is stressful and tiring and means that we are unlikely to be at our best.*"

- We can try to build in at least a minute or two for ourselves between tasks or clients. This will allow us to (eg) make notes on the session, to recall important aspects of the next client's current circumstances, and to take a short time out period. Even a minute or two spent alone between clients can be very refreshing.

  The risks of overload are not difficult to understand. Working behind schedule is stressful and tiring and means that we are unlikely to be at our best. We may become impatient and less tolerant. Being behind schedule also means that people are going to be kept waiting, and this often leads them to complain and to feel, even before they meet us, that we are not giving them sufficient consideration. If, on top of that, we appear impatient and rushed when we do see them, they may become vexed and challenging. And we, of course, will not be in the best frame of mind to deal with any antagonism in a calm and safe way.

- If we know, for example, that we are at our best in the mornings, we try to schedule our most difficult tasks for that time. We don't try to deal with our most demanding tasks at a time when we are at our least alert and our least energetic.

- If we know that a particular client is always difficult or drunk in the afternoons, try to schedule him or her for the mornings.

4. CONSIDER HAVING A PERSONAL ALARM

- We may find that our employer issues them on request. If not, we may feel that such an alarm would be a very worthwhile investment for safety in both the work place and in non-work environments. If we do have a personal alarm we should test it in our workplace. Demonstrate to colleagues the sound it makes, experiment to find out who can hear the

- alarm when we set it off at various locations, *and agree what the response will be.* Thereafter, don't "cry wolf"; the last thing we want is for our colleagues to think we are joking, on the one occasion that we operate it in earnest.

- Personal alarms can be used very effectively in small organisations, providing there is an agreed response when they are heard. Some people place them rather like fire-extinguishers, taping them to specific locations, say one just under the desk, another by the reception hatch, and so on. This gets over the problem of being unable to think where our alarm is, just when we need it; it is always in a fixed position.

5. CONSIDER BEING 'EX-DIRECTORY' AT HOME

- Partly because clients may take to phoning us incessantly at home, but mainly because

- By looking up our name in the telephone directory, they will be able to learn of our address. When someone issues a serious threat to us, or to our family, it is reassuring to know that they cannot easily find out where we live.

6. WOULD IMMUNIZATION BE APPROPRIATE?

- Those working with certain client groups, particularly those injecting drugs, should seriously consider whether they run a risk of contracting a serious disease - such as hepatitis - and should therefore be immunised.

- Some agencies arrange for those who deal with high-risk clients to be immunised, or we may find that the service will reimburse us for immunisation by our G.P.

7. LOOK FOR APPROPRIATE TRAINING

- Take advantage of any training opportunities that are offered. The present programme provides one example of training in safety with clients, and it may be supplemented by linked or separate workshop sessions. Find out, in addition, whether there is any training on offer in breakaway techniques (physical escape techniques used when someone is grappling with us) and control and restraint (this will include techniques for holding off and controlling an attacking client).

- We might also consider undertaking training in first aid.

What safety-relevant training is available to you?

How would you find out about training opportunities within your agency?

Would your agency support outside training in first-aid or other safety-related aspects eg. in terms of time off or fees?

That brings us to the end of the section on personal precautions. We go on now to consider the precautions which may be taken in particular work settings.

The idea is that you should read through ALL of the material that follows, and also pay special attention to the sections concerning the settings in which you work for all or part of your employment, i.e.

- in offices.

- in hospital ward settings and in residential homes.

- when visiting someone at home.

- when escorting clients between locations, eg., in a car.

And finally we complete our look at precautions by considering some general issues regarding the precautions that should be taken at organisational level.

CHAPTER 2:1.3

PRECAUTIONS FOR THOSE WHO WORK IN OFFICES

Here are some precautions for those who see clients in an office situation. This will include such people as probation officers, housing officers, and perhaps nurses and those who work in residential settings.

1. DON'T SEE A POTENTIALLY VIOLENT CLIENT WHEN YOU ARE ALONE IN A BUILDING, either in your office or elsewhere.

2. MAKE SURE THAT THE PERSON CONCERNED IS AWARE THAT YOU ARE NOT ALONE IN THE BUILDING.

Someone who knows that there are other people around will understand that if we are threatened we will be able to call for help.

3. TELL COLLEAGUES IF YOU ARE ABOUT TO SEE A HIGH-RISK CLIENT and agree in some detail what they should do in a range of eventualities. We may arrange for a particular colleague to keep an eye on us, for example by looking in at a window to our office regularly.

One course participant told us how, because she was about to see someone she felt might be aggressive, she left her office door ajar so that her colleagues might hear anything untoward and come to assist if necessary. In due course, a commotion did develop, and a colleague duly arrived and put his head round the door and said: *"Do you mind if I close this door - we can hear every word you are saying, right down the corridor."* Before she could reply, he was away and then went off to lunch with her other colleagues. Eventually, the client barricaded the door, and the professional was taken hostage for several hours.

4. HAVE A PERMANENT SYSTEM FOR CHECKING ON EACH OTHERS SAFETY.

Rather like 3 above, but on a permanent basis. Make sure everyone knows what they should do if they hear a disturbance coming from another office. Some people devise a coded message. For example, if we phone a colleague to ask them to *"Please bring in some cigarettes"* this could be an agreed code for: *"I'm having difficulties, please come to my office immediately"*.

5. PREVENT WAITING TIME AS FAR AS POSSIBLE

People who are kept waiting often become agitated. If we have to keep them waiting beyond an appointed time, make sure to give an explanation. If the client judges that we are keeping them waiting for no good reason, because we are having coffee for example, they are likely to become angry.

Attempt to change their appraisal by offering an explanation such as *"There's been a bit of an emergency today and we're a bit behind, I'm afraid"*. Reception staff are often subjected to abuse and threats when they simply report *"She's busy"* or *"He'll see you as soon as he can"*.
They should be encouraged to phone and say that the client has arrived and is waiting. A further phone call from reception should be taken as a signal that the client is probably somewhat agitated.

The client will find waiting time less irritating if the decor is pleasant, if the seating is comfortable, and if some provision is made for engaging in some pastime.

6. TRY TO PREVENT UNWARRANTED INTERRUPTIONS WHILE YOU ARE SEEING THE CLIENT.

It may be necessary for us to be interrupted occasionally, by colleagues popping in or by telephone calls, but such interruptions can be an irritating distraction both for us and for the client. Consider asking the switchboard to intercept calls, and consider having an 'Engaged' sign to place outside our door.

7. ARRANGE FURNITURE APPROPRIATELY AND DIRECT CLIENT TO THE APPROPRIATE SEAT.

Guidelines concerning 'office layout' are discussed in the next section of this Module. When we have decided which is to be our seat and which is to be the client's, we should make sure that we direct the client to the appropriate chair.

8. REMOVE DANGEROUS OBJECTS (POTENTIAL WEAPONS)

Think about which objects in the office could be used as weapons. Heavy ash-trays, especially if they have sharp edges, are especially **HIGH-RISK**, but vases, mugs, etc. can also be used as missiles. Don't have a knife used for opening letters on view.

CHAPTER 2:1.4 SPECIAL SECTION

OFFICE DESIGN AND LAYOUT

The overall aim in designing an office is to create an atmosphere which is non-oppressive and conducive to ordinary, calm conversation.

Any office in which we see clients should have, ideally:

- *A pleasant decor and a choice of seating*

- *Easy access, in and out, for you, your client, and help*

- *A window so that colleagues are able to look in on you*

- *Telephone contact to other rooms, or an alarm*

- *Absence of potential weapons*

Let us look at some of the relevant issues in a little more detail.

1. ARRANGING THE FURNITURE

- On balance, it is probably best to have a desk in the office because some people actually prefer to be interviewed across a desk. On the other hand, some people don't like being interviewed in such a formal way (and we may feel that in some cases such formality will prevent our interaction with the client from being friendly and relaxed). The fact that there *is* a desk doesn't mean that it has to be used for every interview with every client.

- Wherever in the room we place the desk, make sure that it does not act as a barrier preventing either our client or us from getting out of the room easily.

- If we are interviewing across the desk, avoid placing the two chairs in a direct face-to-face arrangement. This is a confrontational position. Place the chairs at something of an angle to one another.

- If space permits, have an easy area on one side of the desk, so that we can come around and join the client. A couple of easy chairs at an angle to one another, and a coffee table somewhere around is a useful, informal and comfortable arrangement. With the choice of a formal across-the-desk interaction or a more relaxed easy-chair interaction we can tailor the atmosphere of the meeting as we feel appropriate. It can be especially effective if, after a period of across-the-desk interaction, we suggest that we both move to the easy chairs. This represents a clear move towards a more friendly form of interaction.

- Having carefully arranged the seating and layout of the room, of course, we must control which chair our client sits in when they enter the office. We can do this by saying, for example: *"Come on in and sit down"* while indicating a particular chair. It is hardly surprising that many clients sit in the wrong chair when simply asked to sit down.

2. EXITS AND ENTRANCES: THE DOORS

- We should ensure that both we <u>and our client</u> are able to leave the office without being hampered or blocked by the other.

  - We do not want to place the client directly between us and the office door; if the client becomes agitated s/he may take advantage of that situation.

  - On the other hand, many clients leave of their own accord once they recognize that they are becoming agitated, perhaps storming out of the room with suitable insults thrown at us. If this should happen we do not want to be in their path.

- If we work in a very security conscious environment then it may be possible for us to have an outward opening door to our office. Some institutions are now being designed with such doors. The advantage is that they cannot be barricaded from inside (with us taken hostage by our client). However, it is conventional for most offices to have doors which open inwards, so we have to take other precautions ...

- If possible, avoid having a Yale-type lock on the door. The problem with such locks is that they allow the client to easily lock both of us inside the room. Even if a potential rescuer comes along with a key to the room s/he will be unable to release us if the client has operated the catch. Once we are both locked inside the office, the client has time to barricade the door by moving furniture.

- It is far better to have a mortice lock i.e. the conventional key hole lock. The only precaution that we then need to take is to ensure that <u>the key is not left in the lock,</u> on the inside. If that were the case then the client could turn the key to lock us both inside, and with the key remaining in the lock no-one would be able to unlock the door from the outside.

- If there is no other window between the room and the corridor, or another office, then the door should have a window panel for colleagues to look in to check on our safety if they hear a commotion. Such a window panel should be made of strengthened glass or Makralon.

3. THE POTENTIAL TO RAISE THE ALARM

- We should try to ensure that every office we use to see clients in has at least a telephone near at hand. Some people argue that it is necessary to have an alarm button as well. We will discuss the use of alarms in Module Four.

PAUSE FOR THOUGHT

 **Although an office should be designed with safety in mind, it is important that it retain a pleasant and informal atmosphere. A room which reflects a 'fortress mentality' is likely to be cold and threatening and will hardly be conducive to a relaxed conversation.**

Having read this account of good office design, think about your own office, or the offices in which you sometimes work with clients, and try to identify any areas in which improvement could be made.

Alternatively, if you rarely work in a office, you might like to think about the environmental design of a specific location where you do work. Use the headings of this chapter to structure your thinking.

Write here the specific location you want to consider:

....

Then complete the next exercise.

EXERCISE 2.1: OFFICE / ENVIRONMENTAL DESIGN

What improvements could you make yourself, simply and without the need for permission or extra resources?

- .

- .

- .

What improvements could you make with special permission or access to further resources?   And how would you go about applying for these?

- .

- .

- .

> *"Many precautions involve modest changes in furnishings .... which can substantially reassure those who are attempting to give their best to the organisation and its clients."*

CHAPTER 2:1.5

PRECAUTIONS IN WARDS AND RESIDENTIAL SETTINGS

1. PLAN STAFFING CAREFULLY

- Staffing levels should be sufficient for the demands of the clients in the particular setting. Staffing levels which are too low will place stress on staff, will lead patients/residents to feel neglected, and will prevent the formation of good relationships between staff members and clients.

- Pay particular attention to the balance between the shifts. *We should aim for a balance not only in numbers, but also in expertise.*

2. ENSURE GOOD HANDOVERS BETWEEN SHIFTS

- There should be adequate overlap time between shifts to allow time for the in-coming staff to be briefed about issues that have arisen, and to allow them time to read reports and updates to client record forms.

- If we have planned our shifts carefully, and there is therefore a good relationship between the two shifts, then this handover will be much more fruitful than it would otherwise be!

3. KEEP FULL, UP-TO-DATE RECORDS OF INCIDENTS AND CLIENTS' PROBLEMS AND REQUESTS

- It is essential to complete an incident report form if there has been as aggressive threat or attack. The attention of all staff should be directed to the report, and a copy of the report should be sent to the line-manager for eventual inclusion in the organisation-wide monitoring system. A note concerning the incident should also be included on the record form of the client(s) who were involved in the incident.

- It is also important that there should be good communication between colleagues regarding any problems, requests or complaints. It is all too easy for a particular staff member to make a promise to someone which other staff, including those on the next shift, know nothing about.

- If clients realize that communication between staff members is poor, they may also use this to manipulate staff members. For example, by inventing a promise or a concession: *"Jill, on the last shift, told me that it would be all right if I went out for an hour".*

  Poor communication adds to the ambiguity of the situation, adds confusion, and can lead to a potentially dangerous confrontation.

4. MAKE CONSISTENCY OF DISCIPLINE A HIGH PRIORITY ...

- If one staff member is particularly lenient on a point of discipline, for example about smoking, or bedtime, this breaks staff solidarity on the issue. A special risk that might follow from this is that another staff member who then tries to uphold the agreed rules is seen by clients as being inflexible and even vindictive. All of these represent offences or transgressions and are likely to lead to anger.

- The staff *as a group* should consider proposals from clients about changing certain rules, and such changes may even be agreed democratically, within any constraints imposed by organisational policy. But one staff member turning a blind eye to existing rules can add to the risks for other staff.

- Consistency should also be maintained in the way in which we treat different clients. An offence often attributed to staff, especially in residential settings, is that of being unfair, *"Why can she do it and not me?"*; *"You always let him get away with it"*; *"It's not fair, you're always picking on me"* are examples.

- It is sometimes very difficult for residents to come to terms with the fact that fairness sometimes involves treating different people differently, because of their different ages, problems, or capabilities, for example. We should obviously try to treat all residents fairly, and to explain if necessary why this might involve treating two clients in somewhat different ways.

5. ... *BUT*, ENCOURAGE FAIR FLEXIBILITY

> *"Fairness sometimes involves treating people differently."*

- Notwithstanding the need for consistency between staff, staff should agree not to be too rigid about enforcing rules. For example, if bedtime has been set at 10.00pm and a vital televised football match is due to end at 10.05pm, then it would clearly be unreasonable to insist that the ten o'clock bedtime rule be imposed.

- Being seen to be reasonable and flexible in this way may have powerful effects in gaining respect and may generate warm feelings that have a lasting beneficial effect on the atmosphere between staff and clients.

6. BE AS AVAILABLE AND APPROACHABLE AS POSSIBLE

- <u>It's easily said, but we should try to reserve some time so that we can be available for patients/residents.</u> This will allow them to voice any problems or complaints at an early stage, before they get to the point of insisting, in an angry way, that we pay attention to them. It also allows time for us to ask them personal, rather than professional, questions, to talk about ourselves so that they recognize that we are a human being as well as a professional, and to build a good relationship. And of course we should try to be fair in distributing our attention and making ourselves available to various clients.

> *"Approachability is probably the single most important element that people value in the professionals who deal with them."*

- Approachability is probably the single most important element that people value in the people who deal with them. For those in residential settings, at least, it's probably even more important than the client's judgement about how efficient the person is at his/her job.

7. CONSIDER ARRANGING STAFF SUPPORT GROUPS

- When staff work together they may or may not form a good team. Good teams have certain characteristics:

  - *they work together well*

  - *they are relatively free from in-fighting*

  - *they have clear rules which all members abide by, whatever their individual feelings*

  - *they have non-combative methods for re-assessing and (if need be) changing the rules.*

Members of such teams share a common sense of purpose. Individual members know their special responsibilities and their role within the group. Roles are flexible so that if one member is absent, for example, another will take over his/her tasks; when the original member reappears then responsibility for those tasks is handed back without difficulty. Furthermore, communication networks within the team are efficient, everyone identifies with the team, and the team presents a united front to others, for example to clients and to management.

Approachability is sometimes the key

If staff who work together in a particular setting are not working well as a team, one of the precautions that might be taken by the organisation is that of addressing the problem of the lack of group cohesion. An external facilitator might be brought in to work with the group. The practice of team building is now well established and can be very effective. The benefits of creating a well-running autonomous team are often very great indeed, and are experienced positively by the group members and by those who have to rely on the team.

Of course, many teams do work reasonably well together, but it is always useful to arrange regular meetings at which team-working as well as service delivery issues are addressed. Such meetings often provide a useful opportunity for differences to be aired, problems to be addressed, and longer-term changes in policy or procedure to be considered.

8. WHEN WALKING DOWNSTAIRS, WALK BEHIND THE CLIENT

This is a simple precaution, but an important one, standard in many places. If we are walking downstairs in front of someone we may be pushed or kicked, whereas this cannot happen if we walk downstairs behind the client.

9. WHEN INTERVIEWING AN INDIVIDUAL CLIENT, MAINTAIN CONTACT WITH OTHER STAFF.

We may sometimes have to take someone aside for a private conversation. Some such meetings might be of a disciplinary nature or we might have to give the client some disappointing information. We need to consider where it is best for us to hold such meetings.

- *If we feel that a situation might blow up, we shouldn't take the person off to an area which is out of earshot of our colleagues. It is possible to hold a private a conversation even when there are other people close by.*

> **"All manner of costs stem from poor team working. Morale may be low, the quality of working life may be poor, stress levels may be high, and the quality of service delivery will be adversely affected."**

- *If we are in the position of embarking on what may become a difficult interaction with a particular patient or resident, tell one or two colleagues so that they can keep an eye on how things are developing.*

10. GIVE CONSIDERATION TO THE PHYSICAL ENVIRONMENT.

Think about the layout of the working environment.

- *Could certain changes in the allocation of particular rooms or areas be beneficial?*

- *Is furniture arranged appropriately, with comfort and safety in mind?*

- *Are there objects lying around which might be used as weapons?*

The section on 'Offices', earlier, includes a discussion of many relevant points.

CHAPTER 2:1.6

PRECAUTIONS WHEN VISITING SOMEONE'S HOME

Research suggests that home visits are one of the more risky forms of client contact. For that reason it is especially relevant to know about what precautions are appropriate.

Many people who make home visits tend to be somewhat neglectful of even the most basic precautions, and yet there are several measures that can be taken which are both effective and straightforward to achieve:

1. NOTIFY YOUR COLLEAGUES WHERE YOU ARE

- Someone in the office should have a good idea where we are likely to be at all times when we are away from the office. We should leave a copy of our diary in the office, or perhaps with reception staff, or the telephone switchboard operator, so if we do go missing people will have a good idea where they might look for us.

2. ESTABLISH A 'CHECKING IN' SYSTEM FOR THE END OF THE DAY

- If we are not planning to return to the office at the end of the day, but are going off duty straight after visiting someone's home, there should be some procedure by which we can check in by telephone, just to let someone in the office know that we have completed our visits safely.

- Frequently used methods include: having a person who is happy to be phoned at home, so that we check in with him/her if the office is closed, or having an answerphone on which we check in. The answerphone is later remotely-interrogated by an allotted person.

3. BE PREPARED TO ASK FOR A COLLEAGUE TO ACCOMPANY YOU

- If we consider that a visit to a particular client might be hazardous we should be prepared to ask for a colleague to accompany us. Such a request would be routine in some work settings. In others it would be unheard of. How easy would it be for *you* to arrange to be accompanied by a colleague?

4. WHEN YOU ARE IN SOMEONE'S HOME, MAKE A MENTAL NOTE OF THE EXITS IN CASE OF EMERGENCY

- As we approach the client's house, we take a note of the general layout. Is the house isolated, or are there people in the street and in adjoining houses? When we enter the house, we make a point of trying to mentally sketch the layout of the house. We think about possible escape routes we could use if the situation were to become dangerous.

5. BE PREPARED TO REASSESS YOUR GOALS FOR THE VISIT

- Sometimes the reason for reassessing the purpose of our visit will reflect who is around at the time or what mood the client is in. A case that illustrates the general principle emerged in one of our workshops. A social worker who was going to tell a young male client that his claim for benefit was being challenged found him at home drunk and in the company of five other young men, all of whom were in various stages of intoxication. She decided that this was not the time to discuss matters and after a short period of time she left.

6. THINK ABOUT WHERE TO PARK YOUR CAR

- This is another aspect of escape. If we park our car facing the blind end of a cul-de-sac, for example, then we may have to make a three-point turn in order to leave the area. By turning the car around before we make the visit, however, we will be able to leave much more quickly.

7. CONSIDER GETTING A 'DOG REPELLENT'

- Many people who make home visits have had at least one confrontation with a fierce dog. Some dogs, whether they be the client's or a neighbour's, might prevent us from making our visit. In some cases an angry client might deliberately set their dog onto us. Effective dog repellents are now available, and if we make home visits we should consider getting one. One type consists of an aerosol which makes a high frequency noise. Our organisation might issue such equipment, or supply it on request.

CHAPTER 2:1.7

PRECAUTIONS WHEN ESCORTING CLIENTS

Escorting is particularly high risk if the client doesn't wish to go to the destination. We should assess, before our departure, whether the client understands the purpose of the trip, and is agreeable to being escorted by us. The following strategies are especially useful when the client is ambivalent about the journey or is disturbed in some way.

1. TRAVEL ON ROADS THAT ARE WELL POPULATED AND LIT

- The risks of us being badly beaten, or being taken hostage, are clearly much lower if we are in a public space.

2. CONSIDER HAVING ANOTHER MEMBER OF STAFF WITH YOU

- Escorting someone who is disturbed is risky, especially if we are on our own. A person who has been in a residential setting for some time may be disorientated by the outside world and may panic in an aggressive way. If there are two of us then there is more chance of being able to calm the client, or to restrain him/her.

3. TAKE SPECIAL CARE WHEN ESCORTING SOMEONE IN A CAR

- This can be risky because the client may try to get out of the car or may interfere with the driver. Child-proof locks are not the perfect solution because there are times when it would be preferable to let the client make their escape. The only real answer is to have a sufficiently powerful escort team. Ideally, when we are with a person we are concerned about, there should be one person driving and at least one colleague with the client in the back of the car.

4. TELL COLLEAGUES ABOUT YOUR JOURNEY.

- We should always let colleagues know about a problematic journey and the timings of it. Arrange a plan of action that could be used if we fail to arrive or to check in. We must of course remember to inform others if we change our plans at the last moment.

CHAPTER 2:1.8

PRECAUTIONS / ENVIRONMENTAL DESIGN IN CLASSROOMS

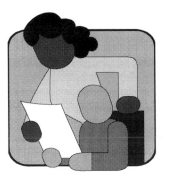

1.   Have clear sight of all pupils.

2.   Pupils should have a clear sight of the teacher/board/display during the whole of the lesson.

3.   Partitions in classroom and work areas should therefore be only of waist height.

4.   Have glass or Makralon panels in the classroom door, and don't cover them with anything, so that colleagues can see if things are out of hand.

5.   Have two adults in the room if this is appropriate.

6.   The teacher's desk should be by the door so that s/he can easily get out to summon help if absolutely necessary.

7.   Particularly high-risk materials (scissors etc) should be stored securely by the teacher's desk with access controlled by the teacher.

8.   Try to ensure that children's routes for accessing materials don't cross each other. Ideally such materials should be stored next to the working area. Establish a routine for fetching and returning materials.

9.   Try to have sufficient working space for each child.

10.   Try to have a quiet/soft area for calming pupils.

11.   Try to use the classroom only for appropriate (teaching) tasks. If a disciplinary-type interview is required, try to do that somewhere else.

12. Try to ensure that pupils' possessions are stored securely.

13. Try to make sure that the classroom is prepared for any activity in advance.

14. Be aware of the physical environment. Ideally, have carpeting to deaden some of the unnecessary noise, a comfortable temperature, good ventilation, sufficient lighting and decoration which is conducive to calm, relaxed work. Demonstrate the pupils' own achievements by having their work on the wall.

15. Be aware of items such as window poles and snooker cues, which can be used as weapons. Some of these are absolutely necessary, but it is as well to minimise such items if they are not needed. Keep them locked away when not required.

16. Be aware of the locks on any rooms which are off the classroom, in extreme cases they can be used to imprison the teacher or to hold him or her hostage. Do not leave keys in such locks. Have yale-type locks replaced by dead locks.

17. Have an agreed system for calling for assistance if this turns out to be necessary.

18. Consider the grouping of pupils to maximise good order and minimise the risk of disruptive incidents.

19. Consider your classroom rules and routine particularly for movement around the room and dismissal at the end of lessons. Ensure these are clear, positive, concise and are understood by the pupils.

CHAPTER 2:1.9

ORGANISATIONAL PRECAUTIONS

Although much can be done, in the way of precautions, by us ourselves, there are considerable constraints on how much we can do without the organisation's blessing. Some of the recommendations made in the above chapters need resourcing by the organisation. An individual, for example, cannot replace a solid door with one that has a Makralon viewing panel; the ease with which we can ask a colleague to accompany us on a home visit may depend on staffing levels and other arrangements.

So, what can an organisation do, in terms of precautions, to help protect staff?

We consider the organisation's involvement in precautions under four headings:

1. PROVISION OF SAFEGUARDS

2. PROVISION OF PRACTICE GUIDELINES

3. PROVISION OF SUPPORT FOR STAFF

4. PROVISION OF TRAINING

1. PROVISION OF SAFEGUARDS AGAINST ASSAULT

A) ORGANIZATIONAL SAFEGUARDS:

- Well maintained client files.

- Clear lines of responsibility.

- A realistic workload on professionals.

- A back-up system, so that one person is able to step into another's shoes during periods of sickness, holidays, and training.

B) ENVIRONMENTAL SAFEGUARDS:

- Offices designed with safety in mind.

- Reception areas separated from individuals' offices.

- Offices and other areas furnished with safety and a pleasant atmosphere in mind. This involves features such as doors, locks, viewing windows, and comfortable seating.

- In exceptional circumstances, the work areas may need to be provided with grilles and non-throwable furniture so that even the most angry client is unable to express his/her feelings in a dangerous way. The problem with such fortress decor, however, is that it might actually increase clients' feelings of anger, by indicating a lack of trust.

- Some resources should be allocated for the provision of reading materials, etc. in waiting areas to relieve boredom.

C) TECHNOLOGICAL SAFEGUARDS:

- Consideration should be given to the issuing of personal alarms and the provision of an extensive panic alarm system.

- If we need to travel to clients' homes, or to travel with clients, we might need to be issued with a portable telephone.

- In some areas of a building it might be advisable to install a closed-circuit television system. But, too often one sees the plea for technology being used as an excuse for not planning a system for looking after oneself and one's colleagues. It is surprising just how much can be done on an entirely low-tech basis.

2. THE PROVISION OF PRACTICE GUIDELINES

The organisation should have agreed procedures that can be implemented when, for example:

- Someone arrives in a drunk or disorderly state

- We (or a colleague) judge that a situation is likely to involve a high risk

- We are (or a colleague is) threatened

- We are (or a colleague is) attacked

Clear policies (developed in consultation with the people working in the particular setting) should be established with regard to:

- The monitoring and logging of staff movements, including check-ins following home visits.

- The procedure if someone fails to check in.

- The involvement of the police following an attack.

- Complaints by clients against the organisation or against particular individuals.

- The recording of any threats or aggressive incidents.

How well do you know the practice guidelines within your organisation?

How would you find out about such guidelines?

If you (or one of your colleagues) had a good idea regarding such guidelines, how would you submit this for a consideration by your organisation?

3. PROVISION OF SUPPORT FOR STAFF

Managers/supervisors should be encouraged (and given time and resources) to give full support to staff with regard to their safety needs. Back-up twinning arrangements should be encouraged, so that everyone knows who they are paired with when they need reinforcement or help.

4. PROVISION OF TRAINING

The following may be provided, as necessary, by the service, and employees encouraged to participate:

- Training in psychological calming techniques, as you will receive in Module 3 of this Manual

- Training in physical control and restraint methods, and also breakaway techniques

- Training in relevant organisational procedures and practices

- Training in first aid

In addition, groups of colleagues working together should be encouraged, and given help and time to:

- Work out a group protection/support plan

- Rehearse emergency tactics at the group level

- Work out individual protection plans

- Rehearse individual emergency tactics

Note: *Real-life rehearsal can sometimes be difficult. In this case - indeed in any case - 'Cognitive Rehearsal' can prove invaluable. This is simply imagining - picturing in your mind's eye - what you would do in specific situations. This is a powerful individual action we can take to make it more likely that we will act in our best interests in the heat of the moment.*

CHAPTER 2:1.10

ORGANISATIONAL PRECAUTIONS: UNDERSTANDING RESISTANCE

The measures in the previous section probably seem sensible, and most of them involve relatively little investment of money or effort. Yet many agencies seem not to assign a high priority to taking precautions against risk to their employees.

Let us consider some possible explanations for this.

1. DENIAL

The organisation may, in effect, have turned a blind eye to the risks faced by staff and may be effectively denying that there is a problem. However, the fact that there has so far not been a serious incident does *not* mean that there is no risk. Too often, agencies rush to action only after a member of staff has been injured. Clearly, it is not sufficient that an organisation should be reactive in this way. It should also be proactive and anticipate that one day an employee is likely to be faced with a highly threatening situation. In any event, most of the strategies outlined enhance morale, everyday practice and teamwork.

2. POOR COMMUNICATION

In some cases the relevant management teams are simply unaware of the risks that employees face. One reason for this may be that staff at the ground level have failed to communicate with management about their fears and about near miss incidents. One answer is to have an active monitoring system, one which periodically surveys employees regarding any threats or aggression they have received from clients. It is of course essential that all incidents of physical aggression be reported to a central office, that inquiries should be made as necessary, and that records should be collated and reported on a regular basis.

3. FINANCE

Although many precautions cost very little, some safety measures could prove very costly indeed. We were once asked to report on the safety features of a house which had been taken over by a local authority for the purpose of housing some twenty highly disruptive and criminally violent young people. The whole layout of the house was most unsuitable and what was need was a costly and radical architectural re-construction of the whole interior of the house.

In times of cutbacks, especially, safety measures may feature rather low on the list of priorities for spending, especially if it is judged that risk of a serious incident is rather low.

4. 'TEMPTING FATE'

Some resistance to taking precautions, at the organisational level, might stem from the idea that engaging in elaborate planning to prevent or deal with a serious aggressive incident somehow represents an admission of defeat. It is almost as if there is a fear that planning for such an eventuality may be tempting fate. Staff, too, may feel that if they take too many precautions they will constantly feel as if they are under siege. There may be a temptation to feel that there is little need to take precautions because if danger does arise then *"I can handle it"* or *"our people can handle it"*. The provision of special locks and panic systems might be taken as an admission that there are some circumstances which cannot be handled well.

It is important for all concerned to recognize the multiple sources of resistance to implementing sensible precautionary measures and to try to overcome such resistance. It is possible to overdo things, to use a hammer to crack a nut, but many precautions involve modest changes in furnishings and fittings, or in procedures, which can substantially reassure those who are attempting to give their best to the organisation and its clients.

CHAPTER 2:2

OUR ATTITUDES TOWARDS CLIENTS

So far in this Module we have been concerned with risk and precautions as they relate to client, situational and environmental factors. Yet we should recognize that some professionals also increase the risk by their own attitudes and behaviour. Some high-risk actions reflect stress, lack of skill, or lack of job commitment. Many also reflect attitudes (to the job, to colleagues, and especially to clients) which are less than helpful and result in behaviour which tends to stir up clients.

In some ways, developing constructive attitudes is regarded as the ultimate precaution.

In the following exercise, you are invited to think about some of the high-risk attitudes that professionals might hold.

EXERCISE 2.2:
UNHELPFUL ATTITUDES TOWARDS *CLIENTS*

 Imagine a work setting similar to your own, and dealing with a similar people. There is only one problem: *the staff in this setting - your colleagues in other words - hold all sorts of attitudes towards clients which are unhelpful and cause the clients to become irritated, troublesome and aggressive.*

Below are the names of your imaginary colleagues. Your task is to invent reasons for the irritation and aggression stirred up by your colleagues by completing the following sentences: (All of the names refer to imaginary STAFF members)

Joe Thorpe often irritates clients by

-

-

Mary Thompson is disliked by many clients because she

-

-

Sue Winters has an unhelpful attitude to clients. She seems to think that they are all

-

-

Many clients complain that Peter Maddocks

-

-

DISCUSSION OF EXERCISE 2.2:

 It's unlikely that any two people would ever identify the same dicey attitudes. One of the main problems with many of these attitudes in that they are held very inflexibly. (People regard them rigidly as 'principles'). Here are some *examples* of attitudes that might prove high-risk:

"Some Clients Need To Be Taught A Lesson"

Although it is necessary to place limits on clients' behaviour, this attitude can lead to the use of punishment, excessive force, and threats. If staff members take a position which is too authoritarian it is likely to cause problems.

"I Always Know Best" (Or "I Must Have The Last Word")

This is an example of a rigid and arrogant way of thinking. It denies the possibility that any client who disagrees may have a point. When a staff member digs their heels in, so may the client, and then trouble and animosity can easily develop.

"I Can Deal With Everyone"

We all need to recognize our limits and also recognize that two people may simply not be compatible. Deciding that a particular client might be better dealt with by a colleague can be a helpful way out for us and the client, especially when a relationship has become stuck in an awkward confrontational rut.

"Give Them An Inch And They Take A Yard"

This is the idea that we can't afford to be flexible. The costs of flexibility are regarded as chaos and anarchy. In fact, giving in on a small point is often highly appreciated and is taken as a sign that the we are human and 'alright'.

"Humour Is Out Of Place In My Interactions With Clients"

The person who takes everything very seriously, who is unable to take a mild joke at their expense, and who comes down heavily on any mild teasing behaviour is likely to be seen by clients as a suitable target for aggression. Humour can do wonders to lighten the atmosphere, and even those who find it difficult to inject a touch of humour themselves should at least respond to others' attempts.

EXERCISE 2.3:

 Specifying high-risk attitudes is one thing. Overcoming them is another. A first step in this direction, however, is for us to recognize any risky or dicey attitudes that we hold. If we are aware that we do hold any such attitudes we should think about them carefully (and perhaps discuss them with friendly colleagues) and see whether we can move away from rigid principles and 'musts'.

But another step we can take is to complete this exercise!

Imagine yourself at work: By chance you overhear a couple of people - colleagues or clients - talking about you. What would you really like to overhear them saying about you?

Put aside all modesty and inhibition, simply put down what would really make your day; be imaginative, use up as much space below as you can, and don't be limited by the number of bullets!

-
-
-
-
-
-
-
-
-
-
-

Next, take some time to read carefully through what you have written, and underline or highlight just <u>three</u> of the attributes. Those can be the ones you concentrate on, and work towards deserving, for the next year or more. Don't be tempted to try to work on more than three; three is plenty.

UNHELPFUL ATTITUDES TOWARDS *AGGRESSION*

Other high-risk attitudes concern not the client but AGGRESSION. Again these might be rigidly held principles which lead us into dangerous areas, or lead us to stay in a situation rather than to take avoiding action or to escape.

Here are some examples:

"Verbal Attack Towards Clients is Permissible"

Professionals sometimes launch into a verbal attack, believing that this is not really aggression. Such behaviour, however, *is* likely to be seen as aggressive by the client who, perhaps lacking the verbal skills to repay us in kind, may resort to physical aggression. It is perhaps best summed up by the adage: *Aggression begets Aggression.*

Next, the *Must* attitudes:

"I must never run away"

"I must never show that i'm afraid"

"I must always remain calm"

"I must always stand up to them"

These attitudes all reflect the principle that the true professional does not respond with fear or annoyance, whatever happens. This principle needs to be challenged. For one thing, such attitudes may lead us to stay too long in situations of escalating risk. For another, if we do try to hide the fact that we are bothered by someone's mounting anger then the client may feel that s/he has to become openly aggressive in order to get the message through. It's also inhuman not to show annoyance in the face of provocation, or fear in the face of threat. The behaviour that we regard as cool may therefore be interpreted as a sign of disinterest and lack of concern - and may also be taken as an indication that we are not a 'real person'.

In general, "MUST" attitudes are things we should be wary about. They tempt us into rigid thinking rather than using our judgement in a difficult situation.

Finally, some of us have the attitude that once a person has become somewhat agitated, it is pointless trying to calm him/her. This again is not true. There are many things which can be done to calm the agitated client, and we will be considering many of them in the next Module.

CONCLUSION TO MODULE TWO

A great deal of ground has been covered in this Module. We discussed precautions we might take on our own initiative, with colleagues, or by the organisation. We considered the special precautions relating to different

kinds of work setting. Finally, we explored some *attitudes* which may increase the riskiness of their interactions with clients.

So far we have considered rather stable aspects of the work situation. We have been concerned to set things up to minimise aggression. In the next Module we move on to consider

what can be done *while we are with someone* to prevent him/her from becoming agitated, or to reduce aggression once it has developed.

NOTES

NOTES

MODULE THREE:

INTERACTING WITH AN AGGRESSIVE PERSON

AIMS:

1. **To consider how we can use *non-verbal behaviours* to calm an aggressive person.**

2. **To consider what we might *say* to calm an aggressive person, both generally and in terms of specific techniques.**

3. **To consider how we might escape from a situation which is in danger of becoming, or has already become, out of hand.**

So far we have increased our understanding of anger and aggression and considered precautionary measures that might be employed to reduce the chance that a dangerous episode will occur. In this Module we concentrate on what we can do to calm down someone who is aggressive, and what to do if we don't succeed.

CHAPTER 3:1

HANDLING AGGRESSIVE PEOPLE: OUR NON-VERBAL BEHAVIOUR

Non-verbal behaviour is a phrase used to label all of the behaviours we show while interacting with other people, except for the 'script' of what we say.

Non-verbal behaviours include:

- tone, accent, pitch and volume of voice

- eye-contact

- facial expression

- posture

- our proximity and angle to the other person

- gestures, and so on.

we communicate a great deal about ourselves (and especially our attitudes and our feelings) by our non-verbal behaviour, which sometimes seems to be even more important than what we actually say. when there is a conflict between verbal and non-verbal messages, most people tend to believe the latter, and proclaim their decision with statements such as: *"He said he would get in touch later, but I know he won't, from the way he said it"*.

Non-verbal behaviour is largely unconscious, as shown by the fact that people are often surprised when they see videotapes of themselves interacting with others.

Although most non-verbal behaviour is unconscious and automatic, we can take control of many aspects of these actions. Actors have to do this all the time. We can improve our non-verbal skills through training or by paying particular attention to what we do. Like other skills (driving, for example) they can be rehearsed and practised until we become proficient and the skill becomes part of our automatic repertoire.

Thankfully, most of us are reasonably socially skilled and make relatively few obvious mistakes in our non-verbal behaviour. But here are a few aspects which merit special consideration in relation to interacting with an aggressive person.

> **Major Non-Verbal Techniques discussed in this chapter:**
>
> - Mood-matching / Vocal tone
>
> - Escaping from a confrontation
>
> - Maintaining normal eye-contact
>
> - Using calming gestures
>
> **Second-Rank Non-Verbal Techniques discussed in this chapter:**
>
> - Mirroring
>
> - Body Buffer zone
>
> - The height of seats
>
> They are discussed in this order, below.

1. MOOD MATCHING AND VOCAL TONE

Mood matching is usually automatic. If someone is happy, we try to be somewhat lively ourselves ... if someone is downcast and depressed, we tend to be more downbeat in our tone of voice. We tend to *match the mood* of the person we are interacting with, at least in general terms.

What then, when someone is angry and agitated? Can we seriously be expected to match their anger? Plainly not; that way lies an escalating conflict.

On the other hand, a show of calmness on our part may well irritate them further. At home many people are all too aware that if their partner is angry and irritated there is one sure way to make them really wild, and that is to be ultra calm!

Whether at home or at work, over-calmness in the face of agitation can come across as superior, uncaring, aloof, condescending. It's almost as if we don't care, or can't be bothered to respond in an active way.

So what *do* we do? The ideal is not to match another person's anger by becoming angry ourselves, but at least to match their anger with *a similar energy level*. So we aim to come over as:

- **Controlled** but

- **Concerned** and involved in what the person is saying.

And this is achieved mainly through our *tone of voice*, and *facial expression*.

EXERCISE 3:1
EXPLORING THE RANGE OF VOCAL TONE

The box below includes a series of brief statements which can be used to explore the effects of changes in vocal tone. Your task is to read each statement (aloud) twice, once with the most pleasant intonation possible and once with the most antagonistic intonation possible. If you try hard you will find that you are able to make even the most negative statement sound friendly and supportive!

> *"Excuse me - could you just move to the next seat?"*
>
> *"I'm going to have to ask you to leave"*
>
> *"There's no way I'd be able to agree to that"*
>
> *"We are concerned about the way in which you deal with the children"*
>
> *"Stop that, please"*
>
> *"Who hasn't managed to do their homework?"*
>
> *"Come with me please"*

By doing this brief exercise we demonstrate something that we already knew - that the same word, phrase or sentence can be said in a whole range of different ways. Depending on the *way* in which it is said, the same statement can sound annoyed, frustrated, condescending, hostile or, on the other hand, sympathetic, considerate and friendly. The lesson is clear - <u>when we are interacting with someone who is angry, we try to use tones that are calming and that convey respect.</u>

2. ESCAPING FROM A CONFRONTATION

A head-on, face-to-face position is challenging and confrontational and is rarely adopted in normal interaction between males in the U.K. (Though it is by females.) *It is, however, the stance adopted by those seeking to be actively aggressive, regardless of gender.*

If we are confronted in such a way, our urgent task is to introduce an angle - even a very small one - between us and the would-be aggressor; this is a very powerful thing to do, because it greatly lessens the sense of, and reality of, threat.

EXERCISE 3:2 Practise by standing with both feet pointing straight ahead and imagining someone aggressively confronting you. Then put your weight onto one foot / leg / hip; this automatically makes the other foot swing out. This in turn tends to move the upper half of your body around slightly and away from the confrontational position. It is only a slight movement, but a crucial one, either you are being confronted or you're not. Practise it in the privacy of your own home!

Note any observations you have, here:

3. MAINTAINING NORMAL EYE CONTACT

The pattern of eye-contact through an increasingly aggressive interchange is as follows:

- Initially there is the 'normal' eye-contact that takes place in any conversation. That is, the person listening looks at the person who is talking roughly twice as much as vice versa. Spells of joint eye-to-eye contact are normally of a limited duration.

- As aggression develops, both parties tend to avoid eye contact. This is probably through an unconscious awareness that eye-contact exaggerates whatever is the ongoing emotion.

- Stage three is where at least one of the people involved - the aggressor - indulges in steady, staring aggressive eye-contact, and will sometimes demand eye-contact from the other: *"Look at me!"*

Our task then, is to do all we can to stay at the first stage - the 'normal' stage, or as close to it as possible. If we are being aggressively challenged we do not want the aggressor to think we are returning the challenge. To some extent this can be done by an effort of will, but there are three things that can help us, when things are getting heated:

> *"Although most non-verbal behaviour*
> *is unconscious and automatic,*
> *we can take control of many aspects*
> *of these actions."*

- We mentioned earlier that it is advisable not to have the chairs directly facing each other. Observational research studies demonstrate that this *is* so, but it is interesting to consider *why* it is. It may be because it is much easier for the would-be victim to occasionally look away if the chairs are at an angle to each other, and maintain the 'normal' eye-contact in a situation which runs the danger of escalating. If the chairs are directly facing, this is much more difficult.

- If we are standing the same thing applies, we try to get a slight angle between us. (See 'Escaping from a Confrontation' above.)

- One ploy is to take notes about the person's grievances. This can be useful because it indicates concern on our part and shows that we are taking the matter seriously, but it also gives us a reason for turning our attention and our gaze successively between the person and our notes.

  Like all such ploys, there are only a few occasions when it is right to use it. However, on these occasions it can be very effective indeed.

When, if ever, might you to use the note-taking strategy?

---

4. USING CALMING GESTURES:

There are many aggressive gestures but few effective calming ones. However, there are two that are effective when used correctly.

The first is where we hold up one, open hand, not vertical, but at about 30 degrees to the horizontal, at about chest height, and then make three or four patting movements at the rate of about 2 per second. It sounds very detailed and contrived, but some people seem to do it automatically and effectively. As they say, spontaneity comes with practice. Sometimes it is done more at waist height, with the hand almost horizontal. In both cases it is non-obtrusive - the aggressor hardly notices it is being done because it is being done so subtly.

The second is where we hold up both hands, open-palmed, almost as though to protect the face, and sometimes we turn the face away somewhat. This is usually a response to real, overt aggression, an imminent attack, but is surprisingly effective.

Have you ever seen either of the two calming gestures above in use? When?

What was the effect?

What would have happened if the gestures had not been used? Could they have been used more effectively ... if so how?

---

5. MIRRORING

When two people are interacting they tend to adopt the same physical position. When one leans forward, the other tends to do the same thing. If two people are standing and one sits down then the other is likely to follow. *Research has shown that people who mirror one another tend to get along better than those who do not.*

Although mirroring is normally an automatic and unconscious phenomenon, we can use the effect deliberately in order to improve the quality of our interactions. As long as we do it subtly, to avoid obvious mimicking, mirroring the way the other person is sitting or standing will tend to make the them feel more at ease.

In addition, adopting another person's posture can often help us to get in tune with the other person's feelings ... it is, after all, very difficult to feel how a slouching person feels if we are sitting on the edge of our seat, and vice versa.

6. BODY BUFFER ZONE

Each of us has an egg-shaped zone around us that we like to keep as our personal space. If someone comes too close, and invades this space, we tend to feel uncomfortable, crowded, and perhaps threatened. It's therefore useful to avoid intruding on an individual's personal space by keeping a reasonable distance from them and allowing them space.

On the other hand, if we are seen to remain resolutely too far away, then we risk being seen as evasive, aloof, stand-offish and rude. So it's another of those 'between two extremes' situations. One special difficulty in getting it right is that different people have body buffer zones of different sizes. There are even differences in the optimal distance across different cultures, e.g. Arabs tend to stand closer that Westerners.

The best policy is for us to err on the side of safety by putting slightly more distance between ourselves and someone who is angry than we would with most other people. One obvious reason for this is that we will then be out of arm's reach; *another reason is that people who are habitually violent have a much larger body buffer zone;* they are more easily 'crowded' than other people.

7. HEIGHT OF SEATS

Everybody knows that when two people are sitting on chairs of different heights, the person sitting on the higher chair seems to be in the superior or dominant position. The person on the lower chair may therefore feel intimidated or annoyed. Actually, it's not quite as simple as that - it depends on a number of other factors. Nevertheless, it's probably best to have two chairs which are at roughly the same height. At least that way we cannot be accused of playing some kind of power game.

SUGGESTIONS FOR PRACTICE ....

The ideal way for you to explore some of the ideas discussed above is to work with another person. If your reading of this course is being supplemented with workshops and discussion sessions you might use these to practise non-verbal behaviours and to experience the effects of mirroring, squaring up, invasion of the body buffer zone, etc.

If you are participating in this course on the basis of this book alone, without supplementary workshop sessions, then consider asking a friend to help you explore some of the aspects of non-verbal behaviour discussed above.

You can explore mirroring even without the knowing cooperation of another person. Make a point of subtly mirroring a friend or colleague within the next day or so, and see whether you can identify effects on (a) the other person's behaviour, and (b) your experience of the interaction.

CHAPTER 3:2

INTERACTING WITH AGGRESSIVE PEOPLE: OUR 'SCRIPT'

So far in this module we have looked at our Non-Verbal behaviour. In this section we consider our 'script' when interacting with an aggressive person.

When we are confronted with someone who is intent on being aggressive - either to us or to someone for whom we are responsible – there are two things we have to do:

    1) **we have to calm them down**

    2) **we have to sort out whatever is upsetting them, *if this is possible***

This is our overall strategy, which we must not lose sight of. We have to be clear what stage we are at, all the time we are talking, for:

- It is no use trying to indulge in logical problem-solving (sorting out whatever is upsetting them) with someone who is hopelessly agitated, and conversely

- Prolonged 'tea and sympathy' is simply likely to inflame the situation, when someone is ready and desperately eager to resolve the problem.

Happily, many people are very skilled both at calming others and at producing solutions (sorting out whatever is causing the aggression). The most common mistakes we come across are therefore either that the first stage is omitted, and we launch straight in to sort the problem out, or that we persevere on stage one, when the person is desperate for some tangible action.

In Chapter 3:2.1 we look at general verbal strategies.
In Chapter 3:2.2 we look at specific verbal techniques.

CHAPTER 3:2.1

OUR 'SCRIPT': GENERAL VERBAL STRATEGIES

Topics Covered in this Chapter:

> **The following topics are covered in this chapter. They are broad approaches, relevant in most situations**
>
> 1. allow the person space and time
> 2. show concern and understanding
> 3. communicate clearly
> 4. convey your desire to reduce distress
> 5. avoid escalating by confrontation
> 6. avoid provocative phrases
> 7. be ruthless with the issue, *gracious with people*

Some of the above are useful mainly in calming the person, others are mainly in the problem-solving stage. Many apply in both. All are described in greater detail below.

1. ALLOW THE PERSON SPACE AND TIME

Someone who is angry often needs to get it off their chest, and anything that conveys the message that we don't have time to listen to their complaint or their worry may inflame them further. So phrases such as:

> *"Tell me exactly what is bothering you"*
>
> *"Let's sit down and talk about this"*
>
> *"What is worrying you about this?"*

give the person space and permission to give their own account. It's important, of course, that we convey our interest and concern by our non-verbal behaviour when they are presenting their account and that we actively listen to, and remember, details of what they say. This will help us in formulating a plan of action.

2. SHOW CONCERN AND UNDERSTANDING

This is done mainly by reflecting back to check whether we have understood correctly, often called 'active listening'. For example, if we say:

"So you wrote first, and then called at the office"

we are letting the person know that we are listening and that we understand what they are saying. Our efforts to grasp the person's predicament also indicate concern and interest on our part and may be reinforced with statements such as:

"I want to make sure that I've understood this properly ..."

In addition, it is a good thing to reflect our judgement of the person's *feelings* both in retrospect,

"You were probably quite angry when they said they hadn't received the letter"

and in the here and now

"I can see that you're very upset"

'Upset' is probably a better word to use than 'angry'. It is more sympathetic, and the person may accept this label and react more like someone who is upset than someone who is angry. 'Put out' is also a useful phrase.

In addition to acknowledging the feelings, it is often possible to sympathize, e.g.

"If I were in your position I would be put out too"

Agreeing that strong feelings are reasonable in the circumstances is a useful way of winning the person over - usually much better than denying that the person has any right to feel that way.

3. COMMUNICATE CLEARLY

Yes, it's obvious that we should be clear in what we say, but this is not always easy. People are sometimes limited in their understanding of social structures (the

relationships between different organisations, for example), of the rules governing particular organizations, and of the roles and responsibilities of people within those organizations. So 'communicate clearly' does not simply mean speak audibly and avoid jargon; it also means avoid making unreasonable assumptions about the people's understanding.

There is a thin line to tread, for if we talk down to a person we are likely to be seen as patronizing and underestimating their intelligence (a serious transgression!) and we may increase their anger.

4. CONVEY OUR DESIRE TO REDUCE DISTRESS

Having acknowledged the person's feelings, we should indicate that we will try to make him/her feel better about the situation. Phrases that can do this include:

"I'm sure we'll be able to sort something out"

"It probably won't turn out as bad as you think"

These phrases encourage the person to calm down by assuring them that some helpful action will be performed, or at least will have been planned. The message we are giving follows the line:

"Your problem is upsetting you at the moment, but we will try to solve this problem ... and there will then be less for you to be upset about."

The hope is that the person will be less angry at the end of their interaction with us not only because of the practical help we are able to offer but also because they have had a chance to put their case, and because this has been carefully listened to (and their feelings acknowledged). They may also feel content because they have found an ally - someone who understands them and is prepared to work on their behalf.

```
Insert a phrase of your own here:



```

5. AVOID ESCALATING BY CONFRONTATION

Again, it's very tempting at times to think:

"I'm right and they're wrong," or

"I can't let them get away with this."

But if we let it become a contest, with a winner and a loser, the situation is likely to escalate and to get out of hand.

Much better then, to use the calming strategies outlined above, and, of course, to attempt to address the person's problem in a constructive and collaborative fashion.

6. AVOID PROVOCATIVE PHRASES

At times it may be very tempting to tell someone who is being unreasonable just what we think of his or her complaint, perhaps by using one of the following phrases:

"Don't be silly"

"I can tell you, other people have far greater problems"

"Pull yourself together"

We all know that this is likely to make matters worse, and so we should make every effort to avoid inflaming the situation with such phrases. All of the above examples amount to telling someone to *"Grow up"*. They are patronizing and demeaning, and to a person who is already angry they may be like a red rag to a bull.

7. BE RUTHLESS WITH THE ISSUE, *GRACIOUS WITH PEOPLE*

There are some times when there is little we can do directly to help the person who is aggressive to us. Police officers making an arrest, Customs and Excise (VAT) officers fining a business person, Social workers taking children into care, Probation officers 'breaching' Community Service workers, and so on.

At such times we need to have a clear distinction between the issue - 'our task' - and the person we are dealing with. Handle the person with the respect and dignity that all deserve, while at the same time being clear that the task in hand has to be completed. Some people call it 'saving face' for the person in question, others just call it respect. Either way, it is summarised by the heading: 'Be ruthless with the issue, gracious with people'.

CHAPTER 3:2.2

OUR SCRIPT: SPECIFIC VERBAL TECHNIQUES

As well as general strategies, there are also a range of verbal *techniques* available to us. The main thing we have to remember with techniques is that *each is only useful in certain circumstances*. So the list below is more like a menu than an instruction: you choose a technique according to the situation, and if one seems not to be working, you might try another. It is as well if we are thoroughly familiar with these techniques, it means we have something substantial to draw on in an emergency.

The 'Menu' of techniques described in this chapter, each one powerful in particular circumstances:

1. depersonalize the issues

2. personalize yourself

3. empower the person

4. make a token concession

5. make a deliberate friendly gesture

6. using "we"

7. using diversions

Each of the techniques is described on the following pages.

1. DEPERSONALIZE THE ISSUE

Most frequent use:

i) where we have to refuse a request

ii) where we have to make happen something the person doesn't want

A probation officer once told the following story against himself. A client came into his office, asking for money *"for the bus home"*.

The probation officer pondered briefly, and said: *"I don't believe you want this money for the bus .. I think you are going to spend it on beer .. so I am not going to give it to you."*

Whereupon the client hit him.

The point he was making, in telling that story, was that he had turned the request into a very personal matter; he had personalized the issue instead of depersonalising it. The only way the client could think of to save face was to hit him. Supposing instead he had said something like:

"Well there are rules about giving out money, and I can't give it out for bus fares, so we are going to have to think about how else you can get home."

It's unlikely that the client would have hit him then.

It's paradoxical that the second version - the 'safe' one - was in fact much closer to the truth of the situation than the first. And this is usually the case; in our jobs we are not normally *personally* responsible for everything, we are acting on behalf of our employers, so we might just as well be straightforward about that.

2. PERSONALIZE YOURSELF

Most frequent use: When we are receiving threats or abuse simply because of our *role* as teacher, nurse, police-officer etc.

Some professionals occasionally receive threats simply because of their *role*; simply because they are a social worker, or a police officer, or a nurse, or whatever.

In those situations, such abuse can often be cut short immediately if we can think of something to say which turns us into a real person, not just a role.

One way of doing this is to give the person some relevant personal information about ourselves. For example:

"That's just what my husband/wife says to me sometimes"

"I know that when my little boy went into hospital, I couldn't sleep. I just stayed awake all night thinking about him"

"When I lost my mother last year ... "

Obviously, it is assumed that the above disclosures would be made only in a context in which they were relevant and where we judged that the revelation might help the person to identify with us.

This is a powerful technique, and research studies have shown that it is one of the most effective things that a potential rape victim accosted by an unknown assailant in the street can do. That is, to say something that transforms them from a fantasy 'victim' into what they really are, a *real person* with a life going on, somewhere they are meant to be, somewhere they have just come from, or whatever.

The most difficult aspect of the technique is to think of information that is appropriate at the time. If we can do it, however, it is liable to work well.

Are there any dangers associated with self-disclosure? What?

---

3. EMPOWER THE PERSON

One imbalance in the professional relationship relates to power. Within the relationship, although maybe not in other areas of their lives, the professional has more access to resources, more knowledge about relevant issues (the law, for example, and agency policies), greater access to important communication channels, and more power to make decisions.

In an ideal situation the client will accept the imbalance without resentment and without challenge, but in certain situations they may become antagonistic and resent the fact that the professional has more power. Such feelings may give rise to an open challenge, and the professional's attempts at resisting this may cause annoyance and increased efforts to undermine him or her, with statements such as:

"Just who do you think you are, telling me how to run my life?"

"You're only a jumped-up pen-pusher anyway"

"You sit on your high horse, trying to push me around"

are clear challenges to our status and authority. If we do dig our heels in and try to meet the challenge head-on there is a real danger that a full-blown battle for dominance will ensue.

In such a situation it can be very powerful if we do something to make the relationship temporarily more balanced. Examples of this strategy are expressed in the following statements:

> *"Well, if you were in my position what would you do?"*

> *"Alright, suppose I came to you with the same problem and you were my probation officer / nurse / etc. - what advice would you give me?"*

This role reversal tactic can be very useful in (a) briefly changing the power balance; (b) putting the person in our shoes (they may then see that an easy solution is not possible); and (c) gaining information about what the person is hoping we will do.

Of course, empowering someone means much more than simply taking a one-down position ourselves. The following statements provide examples of messages that are likely to make a person feel stronger and to motivate them to work at solutions to their own problems:

> *"I think you've got the strength to sort this one out."*

> *"You're a survivor, Jean. You've handled big problems yourself in the past. Now I'd like to help you to deal with this one."*

The message coming through in such statements is: *"I respect your power and recognize your strengths and I'm hopeful that you can succeed in overcoming your problems."*

4. MAKE A TOKEN CONCESSION

When a person is angry with someone else, and makes a sharp complaint, they usually expect a defensive response; one which aims to put the blame back on to them. This naturally results in a sort of duel between the parties, with both unwilling to back down. Such duels can suddenly come to an end, however, if one or other party makes a slight concession. In some conflict training courses this is referred to as the '1% technical error strategy' - one party makes a slight admission of guilt.

The point is not to give in or sell out. What is involved is a *token* concession used deliberately in order to break the *"I'm 100% right and you're 100% wrong"* message which tends to come from both sides. What often happens is that when one side yields just a little, the other one does too, and a pattern of cooperation develops to replace the antagonistic escalation.

Phrases that are useful in making a token concession include:

> *"I see you do have a point."*

> *"Clearly, something has gone wrong somewhere."*

What sort of thing might you say as a 'token concession'?

---

5. MAKE A DELIBERATE FRIENDLY GESTURE

Another way of breaking a conflict situation is to meet antagonism with a friendly gesture. Angry people are often calmed rather dramatically when the person they are angry with offers them a 'gift'. The 'gift' might be time, some form of special consideration, or something material. And it may (again) be a mere token. Take the following statements:

> *"Come into the office and we'll sit down and talk about it."*

> *"Would you like me to phone the housing people for you?"*

> *"I can give you some leaflets that might help."*

> *"Let me get you a cup of tea"*

It's not really important what the gift is, but the fact that we are offering something puts us in the donor role. *When we are giving or offering something, there is a kind of in-built response which makes the recipient feel grateful to us.* And it's difficult to be grateful to someone and annoyed with them at the same time.

6. "WE ...."

'We' is a very significant word, conveying ideas of partnership and collaboration. Emphasizing that *'we'* need to find a solution to the problem reduces feelings about the power difference and it stresses collaboration.

After a very serious hostage incident in which several people had been shot, and two had been killed, an interviewer spoke to the perpetrator, and asked him why he had not killed Bruce, a hostage who was being made to drive the bus they were on. (From the details of the incident, we would have expected that the perpetrator would have killed him; indeed he had the gun to his head at one point.)

His reply was: *"It was the way he looked at me* ...and he said 'We' ... he said, 'We ain't never goin' to getaway with this, bro' ...".* The perpetrator looked wistful even at the recollection, as though remembering the feeling of camaraderie. Bruce had demonstrated that he was somehow on the perpetrator's side ... Why harm a person who is on your side?

> *"Emphasizing that 'we' need to find a solution to the problem reduces feelings about the power difference and it stresses collaboration."*

(*Making eye-contact is one of the simplest means of personalising ourselves. (See earlier.) In many thoroughly-planned hostage-takings and kidnappings the perpetrators now hood their victims, to prevent this taking place.)

7. USING DIVERSIONS

The idea here is a simple one: when someone is being aggressive, either to us or anybody else, we try to divert their attention, usually on to something more appealing. As one foster-carer put it: *"Whenever my two girls are fighting with each other I just get out the Monopoly Board."*

There are dangers of course, because we are in a sense 'rewarding' the aggression. In the example above, the girls may well have learned that an easy way of getting their carer's attention for the evening is to start a vicious quarrel. Even so, 'Diversion' can be an effective *short-term* measure, and there are times when we are happy to leave worrying about the longer term until later!

EXERCISE 3:2

The list below summarises the 21 topics we have covered so far in
this chapter. Read through the list, check you know what each
topic is, and put a tick by those that you intend to use from time to
time. Remember, many of them are not confined in their use to
aggressive situations, they can improve our practice generally.
Place a tick in the appropriate box, even if you already use the technique in
question; you might be signifying that you intend to extend its use in future.

Non-Verbal Techniques

1. mood-matching / vocal tone   ____
2. escaping from a confrontation   ____
3. maintaining normal eye-contact   ____
4. using calming gestures   ____
5. mirroring   ____
6. body buffer zone   ____
7. the height of seats   ____

Broad Approaches, relevant in most situations

1. allow the person space and time   ____
2. show concern and understanding   ____
3. communicate clearly   ____
4. convey your desire to reduce distress   ____
5. avoid escalating by confrontation   ____
6. avoid provocative phrases   ____
7. be gracious with people, ruthless with the issue   ____

Specific Verbal Techniques

1. depersonalize the issues   ____
2. personalize yourself   ____
3. empower the person   ____
4. make a token concession   ____
5. make a deliberate friendly gesture   ____
6. using "we"   ____
7. using diversions   ____

CHAPTER 3:3

ESCAPE

There are times, albeit rare, when someone's behaviour really does get out of hand. There comes a stage when efforts to calm the situation have failed and our major concern is to escape and, possibly, to raise the alarm or to seek help. In such circumstances we should gauge whether other people (other clients, for example, the public, or other professionals) are likely to be threatened, and we should try to ensure that we are not leaving a dangerous person on the loose.

The simplest way to escape is simply to leave, just go, if you think you can. After all, when our physical well-being is in jeopardy, good manners come second. This may be particularly the case if we work mainly in 'open' situations, out of doors. However, especially if we work in offices or interview rooms, we may wish to make an excuse to leave and, if so, this can be done in a number of different ways. For example:

- **Tell the person that, because you are both on edge, it would be better to resume at another time. It helps if we suggest another specific appointment.**

   eg: *"Come on, we're not really getting anywhere now ... let's take a break and see if we can sort it out this afternoon."*

   What might you say? Write it here:

- **Tell the person that we are going to fetch a colleague who may be better placed to help.**

   eg: *"Look, the best person to sort out housing benefit is Mrs Smith ... you stay here and I'll go and get her."* (Whether you actually get Mrs Smith is immaterial is this case, you may or may not. Your priority is to get out and get help.)

   What might you say? Write it here:

IF THE PERSON REFUSES TO ALLOW YOU TO LEAVE, OR PHYSICALLY BLOCKS YOUR PATH, THEN THE SITUATION HAS BECOME MORE DANGEROUS.

Nevertheless there are still a number of options, which this chapter describes.

The topics covered are:

1. Play For Time
2. Keep Talking
3. Diversionary Tactics
4. Maintain Distance
5. Stay Controlled and Concerned
6. Locate And Move Towards Escape Exits
7. Tell the Person To Put Any Weapon Down
8. Delayed Compliance
9. Consider The Use Of Physical Restraint

---

1. PLAY FOR TIME

Curiously, even in the most extreme and well-planned scenarios, an aggressor will normally only harm his or her victim in the first few minutes of an interaction, if at all. In such an extreme situation, therefore, our aim is always to buy time, at almost any cost ... normal priorities are suspended, normal ideas such as *"I mustn't promise things I am not absolutely sure I can deliver"* are put on hold.

- When the going gets tough, don't insist on maintaining your authority, and don't be afraid of *appearing* to lose face.

- If there is a knife at your throat (metaphorically or - it could happen - in reality) then say anything, promise anything. This is equivalent to the instruction given to bank, building society, and post office employees - *"If you are held up with a weapon, hand over the money"*.

- Promise the Earth, if need be *("I'll have your children back with you within an hour", "I'll make sure that by this time tomorrow you have a house of just the type you want")*. Promises made under such extreme circumstances are clearly not morally binding, and we won't have to deliver the goods.

2. KEEP TALKING

Keep talking, using our normal tone of voice to encourage mood matching. Silences can be threatening, and by continuing to speak we keep the initiative. It can help us to stay in control.

Additionally, asking *relevant* questions can seem to put us back in control. The person asking questions usually appears to be the one in control. However, in a highly charged situation, the questions need to be highly relevant if we are to have a chance of them being answered. For example, if we are talking to a man who is distraught because his wife has disappeared, we might be asking:

> *"Has she gone missing before?"*

> *"Has she taken clothes with her?"*

> *"Has she got a close friend she might have gone to?"*

and so on, obviously pausing between each one for the person to reply.

Notes, and possible occasions you could use this:

---

3. TRY DIVERSIONARY TACTICS

There are various ways of trying to break out of a situation which has become locked. These include:

a) Humour

At this stage humour can be dangerous, especially if the aggressor feels that we are laughing *at* him/her or that we are treating his/her problem in a less than serious way. Humour can help, however, if we are sure that it will come across as a good-humoured attempt to break the deadlock.

The most effective humour in such dangerous situations tends to be self-deprecating, as in the following examples:

"I guess it's just not my day"

"And I thought it was going to be a boring day today"

"We don't really seem to be getting along all that well, do we?"

Hardly classic one-liners, but they may serve to break a charged atmosphere.

b) A Distracting Activity

Where the situation has become highly aggressive and deadlocked any suggestion involving doing something may be sufficient to break that deadlock.

Examples of such suggestions include:

"Why don't we take a break, let's go and get a cup of coffee from the kitchen."

"Listen, why don't you call your wife and talk it over with her, and then come back and we'll discuss what she says?"

c) The Novel Question

Sometimes a deadlock can be broken if we make a statement, or ask a question, that is at a tangent to the present situation. For example, if the person's predicament concerns housing, or child protection, and we are trapped in our office, asking a question such as *"How did you get here today?"* or *"How many times have you been to this office?"* will add a little confusion that may actually help to resolve the situation. The idea is that the aggressor will be too busy thinking about why we have asked that particular question to maintain his/her single-mindedness about keeping up a high level of threat.

And again, the questioner often seems to be in control, even if the questions are asked gently.

d) Feigning Distraction

Feigning distraction is a very powerful technique of throwing a spanner in the works. All social situations (including highly threatening ones) have a kind of rhythm. Both players in a two-person interaction have a fair idea about what is going on and what is likely to happen next. Feigned distraction suddenly breaks the rhythm and once a rhythm has been broken there is a kind of dislocation, and things may settle into a new, less threatening, pattern.

That's the theory. Now here is what we do.

We suddenly 'start' as if we have heard something beyond the room, or, alternatively, we pretend to start at something we have seen through a window. Typically, we would hold our hand up, as if calling for silence. This stops the current interaction dead, while we look puzzled and give every indication that we are straining to listen or to see clearly whatever has distracted us. After a couple of seconds or so (and it usually *seems* much longer), we give some explanation.

For example, "I'm sorry, I thought I heard someone shouting" or "Sorry, it looked like my car for a moment").

The aim of the feigned distraction is not to simply buy time of a few seconds or so. The power of the technique is that it disrupts the on-going interaction in a very dramatic way. This disruption can then provide a turning point, a change of gear, so that the previous level of confrontation and aggression is sharply reduced. This technique, of course, can be used only once in a situation. Also, we should practise it at least a few times, with friends perhaps, or our partner, so that we can observe the way in which it disrupts on-going interaction. *Feigning distraction is not a first-line technique, but it may be a useful one to have up your sleeve if things are becoming seriously threatening.*

Notes, and possible occasions you could use this:

4. KEEP OUR DISTANCE

There are a number of good reasons for maintaining a good distance between us and the angry person. For one thing, if we stay out of arm's length, they will not be able to land a punch or a slap, and will not be able to scratch us.

Another reason is that if we stand too close we run the risk of crowding the person, which s/he may find threatening. It is suggested that aggressive people often have body buffer zones which are considerably bigger than those of other people.

5. STAY CONTROLLED AND CONCERNED

We try to give the impression that we are still in control of ourselves. However, remember that appearing too calm can incense a person who is very agitated. There are situations in which it is better to be open and to admit that we are feeling vulnerable. If we judge that it is appropriate, we might use a statement such as the following:

> *"I wish you'd stop pacing around like that, it's really worrying me."*

The very 'openness' of the statement makes it a very assertive one which can be extremely effective when used in the right circumstances.

Notes, and possible occasions you could use this:

6. LOCATE AND MOVE TOWARDS ESCAPE EXITS

When we have decided that we must escape from the confines of the space in which we are being threatened, we should survey the room or waiting area, etc. with a view to moving towards escape exits. It hardly needs to be said that we do this covertly. Consider carefully whether any door is likely to be locked, and think about where the exits lead. Any attempt to make a run for it which meets with a locked door may well escalate the danger. We should plan to escape to a space where there are sure to be some other people around who will be able to help if we are followed or chased.

Notes, and possible occasions you could use this:

7. TELL THE PERSON TO PUT ANY WEAPON DOWN

When a person has a weapon in their hand, be it a manufactured weapon such as a knife or gun or some implement that they are treating as a weapon, such as an ashtray or a chair, we firmly and repeatedly direct the person to put the weapon down. We try to make it clear from our tone that their possession of the weapon is totally unacceptable and they *must* put it aside before our normal interaction can resume. We repeat ourselves endlessly if we have to, use hand gestures to direct them to put the weapon to one side, and - of course - keep our distance. Our vocal tone should be urgent and insistent. The script might go something like this (there would be pauses between sentences):

"Put the knife down, John ... Put it down ... We can't talk while you're holding a knife ... Put it down ... Put it on the table over there ... We can't do anything until you put that knife away ... Put it down now, go on ... put it down, and then we can talk ... We'll sort things out just as soon as you put that knife away ... Put it away now ... Put it on the table ... Come on now, just put the knife on the table ..." (etc.)

We do NOT tell the person to give us the weapon, for two reasons:

- They would be most unlikely to agree to this, because it is like handing over their badge of authority, involving considerable loss of face.

- If they did, it would be dangerous. They are holding the handle so what do you hold? What if the person changes their mind at the last moment?

Notes, and possible occasions you could use this:

8. DELAYED COMPLIANCE

Just as one's daughter can - and does - say *"Dad, in about quarter of an hour, do you fancy a game of cards"* if she sees that 'Dad' is engrossed in something else, or diners in a restaurant will say to a busy, passing waiter *"When you've got a moment, can we have some more drinks here please"*, delayed compliance, as the technique is termed, can have a rather more serious and very effective application.

In one serious hostage taking, where two people had already been killed and two children on the hijacked bus were crying and screaming, the negotiator said to the perpetrator over the radio-phone something along these lines:

"Look, I'm going to ask you something now, but I don't want you to give me an answer straight away, just think about it for a bit. I'm going to ask you to think about letting go of those two kids who are crying and wailing in the background. There's plenty of other folk on the bus after all, and those two kids are doing you no good. Just have a think about it for a quarter of an hour or so and I'll get back to you then and we can talk about it."

By this means - delayed compliance - the negotiator ensured the release of the two children in exchange for a hot drink. Whatever the situation, the essence is always the same: you ask for a particular behaviour to happen in a specified time.

How might you use delayed compliance?

9. CONSIDER THE USE OF PHYSICAL RESTRAINT

At some stage we may have to consider whether it would be possible and appropriate to use physical restraint. This is very much a last resort for a number of reasons. An unsuccessful attempt at restraint is almost bound to escalate the aggression. And in some cases an attempt at restraint will actually cause injury to the aggressor. Apart from the obvious humanitarian issue, any injury caused in this way, however slight, is likely to lead to a formal complaint being made.

> **Think about one or two areas in which you normally see people.**
>
> **Think about possible escape routes.**
>
> **Do you always know which doors are locked and which are not?**
>
> **Do you know where every door leads? How well do you know the layout of your workplace?**

The decision about whether or not to make an attempt to physically restrain someone should be based on a number of factors. We should judge the likely success of such an attempt, bearing in mind the person's physique, age, etc. However, we should remember that whereas those of slight build may be relatively easy to restrain they may also be especially vulnerable to injury if excessive force is used. The most important factor, however, concerns training. If we have attended appropriate control and restraint courses, and have kept in training since, we may be knowledgeable about special holding techniques which are effective and safe. If we have not had such training, there are considerable dangers involved in having a go and that this should be avoided except in dire circumstances.

> *"A professional under attack who attempts to use physical restraint as a self-defence action may suddenly find that s/he is being branded the aggressor, with the aggressor as victim!"*

We have now covered a number of important strategies which may help us to escape from a situation which is getting out of hand. Some of these will help us to physically remove ourselves from the situation whereas others will merely change the situation so that it becomes less threatening.

Remember, also, that the simplest way to get out of a dangerous situation is to leave, and that if all else fails we should call for help. This will be discussed in the next chapter.

CHAPTER 3:4

WHAT TO DO IF YOU ARE ATTACKED

Aggressive incidents *do* happen; not often, but too often nevertheless. Taking precautions can lower the danger level, and we can help to further reduce the risk by the way we interact with an aggressive person. But what if things get out of hand - what is the best way to respond if the person does become violent?

First, we should try to escape. Tell the attacker that you want to go; tell him/her to let you out of the room. Tell the attacker that we want to summon help. If we do manage to leave the room, raise a general alarm. But if our attempt to escape should fail ...

1. TELL THE PERSON TO STOP THE ATTACK.

For example, tell the aggressor loudly and firmly (shouting):

> *"Stop that - NOW"*

> *"Take your hands off me"*

and keep doing so until it takes effect.

2. CALL FOR HELP

By the time things have got to this stage, using the telephone or radio will probably be impractical. Nevertheless, there are other ways:

- **Shouting.** Either just making so much noise so that someone comes to investigate, or if there are other people around, shouting for assistance. *"Come here and help me ... yes you ... come and help me"*

- **Screaming.** If you scream loud enough you can probably make enough noise to stop the aggressor in his or her tracks. You will probably also attract the attention of colleagues or someone you can get to help you. The problem is that many people are embarrassed at the idea of screaming, and wouldn't do it if their life depended on it. You can get over that to some extent by cognitive rehearsal ...

  Break off reading for a minute, and just *imagine* screaming as loud as you possibly can. That might just save your life.

- **Use Your Personal Alarm.** The effectiveness of a personal alarm depends on other people being present, hearing the call, understanding the call i.e. not dismissing it, for example, as a car burglar alarm, and knowing how to respond. How loud the alarm is, and where you are using it, will also alter the degree to which sounding a personal alarm is useful. Importantly, however, the sheer volume will sometimes stop the would-be assailant in their tracks. *But the principal question is, have we got together with our colleagues and agreed what to do if a personal alarm is heard?*

- **Use The Panic Alarm System.** If we have a panic alarm button either on our person or in the room, pressing this should ensure that help is soon on the way. Some rooms are equipped with a silent alarm system; pressing a button may, for example, cause a light to flash in the reception area. *The effectiveness of that, however, will depend on there being agreed and rehearsed procedures.*

- **Use The Fire Alarm System.** If there is no special panic alarm system connected to our room, there may at least be a fire alarm. Use that. Curiously, in the heat of the moment some of us seem to say to ourselves *"No. it's not a fire, so I can't press the fire alarm."* In reality, any alarm is better than no alarm.

3. USE BREAKAWAY TECHNIQUES

If the person is holding us, attempt to break away from them. Numerous breakaway tactics work, and these are taught on special training courses.

4. USE PHYSICAL RESTRAINT

Normally, we should attempt to physically restrain someone only if we have been specially trained in control and restraint methods and feel confident that we will be able to gain the upper hand and be able to hold the person safely.

There are two dangers associated with the use of physical restraint methods. First, an unsuccessful attempt will be seen by the person as a bid to molest him/her, and may well be painful. The level of their violence may escalate. Think why, in terms of the Aggression Incident Model, this would be so. The second danger is that by using inappropriate forms of restraint, such as sitting on the person's chest, we may injure them. Such an occurrence might result in a very ugly situation in which WE are depicted as the aggressor, with the other person as victim.

The answer to both of these potential problems lies in our having received training in the correct methods of physical control and restraint.

CHAPTER 3:5

WHAT TO DO IF A COLLEAGUE IS BEING ATTACKED

1. Spread The Alarm

If we are responding to a help call, then before we do anything else spread the alarm. Let at least one other person know that our colleague is in trouble *before* we attempt to help. This avoids a situation developing in which both we and our colleague are held at knife-point, for example, without anyone else knowing. Tell the person we are alerting to send for the police if necessary. If you are the police, then you will be thinking in terms of requesting back-up.

2. Go To Your Colleague's Assistance

Try to assist your colleague as soon as possible. However, avoid rushing in in a state of near panic. Remember that our mere presence may help to calm the situation, but that this is more likely if we respond in as low key a way as possible. If your colleague is in a room and you find the door locked, let someone know this. Try to find a duplicate key.

Once in the situation with our colleague ...

3. Tell The Person To Stop The Attack

In a commanding tone, tell the aggressor firmly :

> *"Let him go NOW"*   *"Pack it in. Stop that"*

and repeat such a statement until it takes effect.

4. Pull Your Colleague Away

If our colleague is being held, we can attempt to break him/her away. The tactics that can be used to pull someone away are variations of the breakaway tactics used to deal with a personal attack, and they may have been included in special breakaway training courses.

5. Use Physical Restraint

Normally, we should attempt physical restraint only if we have been specially trained in control and restraint methods and feel confident that we will be able to gain the upper hand and be able to restrain the person safely. Remember that an unsuccessful attempt may serve to escalate the level of violence and that inappropriate forms of restraint may injure the person.

We have now come to the end of the third Module. Just one to go!

There are techniques for most situations

Subtle Mirroring has a powerful effect

A token gift is sometimes effective

If all else fails, distraction sometimes works

The fourth Module begins with the psychological aftermath of aggressive threats and attacks, and includes a discussion of various ways in which a victim can be helped after an aggressive incident has occurred.

NOTES

NOTES

MODULE FOUR:

POST-INCIDENT

AIMS:

- **To understand the effects that can follow an assault**

- **To learn how we can lessen the effects after an assault against ourselves**

- **To learn how to help a friend or colleague who has been assaulted**

- **To learn what a manager can do following an assault on an employee**

CHAPTER 4:1

PSYCHOLOGICAL REACTIONS TO INCIDENTS

This section concerns the psychological effects of having been attacked or seriously threatened. The first exercise asks you to recall, or imagine, such effects. You may have been attacked yourself, or have been in threatening situations, or you may know of attacks on your colleagues. You can draw upon all of these experiences in completing this exercise.

EXERCISE 4:1
PSYCHOLOGICAL AFTER-EFFECTS ON THE VICTIM

What do you KNOW or REMEMBER or IMAGINE to be the psychological after-effects for the professional involved in a threatening or violent incident IN THE WORKPLACE?

 Write down in the spaces below the psychological effects that a professional might experience following an attack, under the two headings: *immediate* and *longer term.*

IMMEDIATE PSYCHOLOGICAL REACTIONS

-
-
-
-

LONGER-TERM PSYCHOLOGICAL REACTIONS

-
-
-
-

DISCUSSION OF EXERCISE 4:1

 There is no universal syndrome of psychological effects following an attack. People respond in different ways and to different degrees. Some will be traumatised by a verbal onslaught, while others may respond even to a serious physical attack with apparent equanimity and resilience. However, in some of these cases the initial response is very different from the later response.

Research into the after-effects of attacks on social workers and health service workers, in particular, has revealed a number of symptoms that often occur. You will probably have included some of these in the list you have drawn up. Some, however, may not come to mind. At the end of this discussion you may feel that you have a better appreciation of the various ways in which a person can respond adversely to an attack, both immediately and in the longer term.

1. IMMEDIATE EFFECTS

In the first couple of hours following an attack a person often experiences a complex mixture of feelings, including:

- tension

- psychological numbing

- physical exhaustion

- anger

- euphoria

Despite these feelings, however, many victims will insist on carrying on as if nothing had happened, seeing people and continuing with other work tasks. Often their insistence, characterized by the phrase 'the show must go on', seems to be a strategy for minimizing the impact of the attack. We will discuss below the question of whether carrying on in this way is always the best thing to do.

2. LONGER TERM EFFECTS

Longer term effects may involve adverse emotional conditions, loss of confidence and motivation, and changes in attitudes and beliefs.

a) EMOTIONAL EFFECTS

Depression
One of the most frequent emotional reactions following an attack is depression, and, like depression caused by other life events, it tends to be associated with feelings of hopelessness, guilt about the incident, and pessimism.

Anxiety
Following an attack, the professional may be highly anxious. Sometimes this is generalized but sometimes it focusses on particular aspects of work. There may be a high level of fear about meeting people, particularly those who share some of the characteristics of the attacker. For a long time after their attack, many people remain apprehensive and wary, and they usually overestimate the risk of a repeat incident.

Flashbacks
Some also experience flashbacks and intrusive memories which are very disturbing and cause severe problems in concentration on the work in hand.

Anger
Once the initial shock has subsided, it is often replaced by anger. The person may be angry with the attacker, with people in general, with colleagues and the organisation, or with themselves.

b) LOSS OF CONFIDENCE AND MOTIVATION

A loss of self-confidence often follows some time after an attack, and the person may find it difficult to exercise judgement or authority. They may judge that the assault was degrading and reflects badly on their own expertise. Sometimes this leads to a loss of professional identity, so that they feel that they are not (eg.) a real probation officer or a real nurse. A series of self-statements of the following kind may occur:

> "The attack proves that I'm not a good (social worker) - because 'good social workers' don't get attacked"

> "Therefore I obviously don't have the right qualities to be a (social worker)"

> "Therefore I'd better opt out of (social work) and find another job."

Each of the above statements might be challenged by an advisor or a therapist. It is not the case that good professionals are never attacked, and an attack does not imply that someone is fundamentally unsuited to the job. But things may appear differently to those who have suffered an assault, and many do, in fact, leave their profession prematurely.

Others do not actually resign, but the fact that they are experiencing burnout may be evident in their withdrawal of goodwill, a reduction of conscientiousness, or poor work attendance. Many teachers, for example, take premature retirement, and pupils' disruptiveness and aggression are among the main contributing factors.

c) CHANGES IN ATTITUDES AND BELIEFS

The psychological aftermath of an attack often includes changes in the way in which the professional views him/herself and the job. Their attitude may change sharply, so that they regard many people as unpredictable and potentially dangerous. Colleagues and managers may be seen as withdrawing support or acting in an antagonistic way, and the agency may be regarded as bureaucratic and self-protective. *On the other hand, some people are pleasantly surprised by the support that they receive following an attack, and they may actually feel more valued and part of an integrated team as a result of the incident.*

d) DENIAL

Some victims attempt to cope with the aftermath of an attack by means of psychological denial and forced forgetting. They make a gigantic effort to put the incident out of their mind and insist that colleagues never refer to it. In some cases this might work without detrimental effects, but the accepted wisdom is that it is better for people to come to terms with what has happened to them. The ultimate goal is to put the event into true perspective - not to deny that it ever happened but to accept that it did happen, there may be lessons to be learned, and that such an incident may never happen again.

Summary of Some Possible Short Term Effects:	Bitterness Anger Intrusive memories of the assault
	Denial/forced forgetting
Tension	Lack of interest in everyday events
Psychological Numbing	Sleeplessness
Physical Exhaustion	Irritability
Anger	Loss of Confidence
Euphoria	Loss of 'vocation'
Nightmares	
Summary of Some Possible Longer Term Effects	Note: It is also worth remembering that some people escape remarkably unscathed from some very serious incidents.
Depression	
Anxiety	

EXERCISE 4:2
COLLEAGUES' REACTIONS FOLLOWING AN ATTACK

 **So much for the possible reactions of the victim. Now what about the reaction of his or her colleagues?** Think of three of your colleagues and write their names on a separate piece of paper. This is to avoid the possibility that one or more of your colleagues might look at this book at some time in the future - they might be disappointed or embarrassed if they saw your answers to this exercise. Write out the three names now.

Assign one of the letters A, B and C to each of these colleagues and write the appropriate letter beside each name.

Now, using your piece of paper as a key, indicate in the appropriate columns below (Column A, Column B and Column C) how you think each of these colleagues would be likely to react towards you if YOU had been attacked.

WOULD THIS
COLLEAGUE ACT ...

	A	B	C
sympathetically	*yes maybe no*	*yes maybe no*	*yes maybe no*
in a 'gloating' way	*yes maybe no*	*yes maybe no*	*yes maybe no*
in an embarrassed way	*yes maybe no*	*yes maybe no*	*yes maybe no*
in a helpful fashion	*yes maybe no*	*yes maybe no*	*yes maybe no*
in an 'over-whelming' way	*yes maybe no*	*yes maybe no*	*yes maybe no*
by avoiding the issue	*yes maybe no*	*yes maybe no*	*yes maybe no*
by avoiding you	*yes maybe no*	*yes maybe no*	*yes maybe no*

DISCUSSION OF EXERCISE 4:2

There are a number of possible learning points in this exercise:

a) it's not easy to imagine how people will react

b) some people are likely to be more helpful than others

c) some colleagues would be less than supportive in their response and might react in unhelpful ways, eg. by avoiding us, or by reacting in an emotionally overwhelming way, or even by gloating.

Of course, this exercise only picks up your own predictions of how three colleagues might react, and if the worst were ever to happen we might find that these predictions were not accurate.

> **"There is a tendency for some colleagues to assign a large part of the responsibility for the incident to the victim, in effect to blame the victim."**

So how *do* colleagues respond following an attack? The research shows that whereas some people who have been attacked report a high level of emotional and practical support from their colleagues, others report that colleagues were less than helpful.

Some colleagues are embarrassed and avoid the issue, some make a meal of it and constantly refer to the incident, and some convey a negative message such as *"You must have been asking for it"* or *"It would never happen to me"*. Many victims report disappointment at the treatment that they received from colleagues and managers following an attack.

It does seem that there is a tendency for some colleagues to assign a large part of the responsibility for the incident to the victim, in effect to blame the victim. They may believe that the colleague was attacked because s/he was inexperienced, perhaps, or because s/he was provocative or handled the episode badly.

Why are some colleagues sometimes so unhelpful and unsympathetic?

One possible reason is that the attack has made them concerned for their own safety and that they need a 'victim blaming' explanation to reassure themselves that they are immune to attack. Effectively they have to choose between the following two possibilities:

- *"It could happen to any of us"*, or

- *"It happened to that person because they are incompetent / inexperienced / provocative etc"*

Many people are frightened by the idea that *'it could happen to any of us'*, so choose the latter.

Knowing that such self-protection processes tend to take place after a colleague has been attacked may help us:

a) to understand the reactions of some of our colleagues if we are ever attacked

b) to avoid reacting in this way if one of our colleagues is ever attacked

There is a good deal to be gained by team solidarity following an aggressive incident, and important lessons can be learned from an attack if colleagues avoid such defensive and blaming explanations   ....

CHAPTER 4:2

SUPPORT FOLLOWING AN ATTACK

Following an attack, the longer-term outcome will depend not only on the nature of the attack, and on the victim's personality and coping strategies, but also on the way in which colleagues and managers respond in the hours, days and weeks that follow.

So what responses will help someone after they have been attacked?

Useful self-help and social support strategies following an attack will be considered under three headings :

    1. SELF-HELP

    2. HELPING A COLLEAGUE WHO HAS BEEN ATTACKED

    3. THE MANAGER'S ROLE

CHAPTER 4:2.1

SELF-HELP

Let's begin this section with a brief Exercise.

EXERCISE 4:3   SELF-HELP FOLLOWING AN ATTACK

 It may be painful to imagine it, but suppose that someone physically attacked you, not quite injuring you, but leaving you badly shaken. Furthermore, let us assume that you have to work for the rest of the day. Bear in mind the emotions you think you would be experiencing at the time. Now answer the following questions:

1. Who would you want to speak to within the first HOUR following the attack?

　　•

　　•

2. Would you wish to keep working for the rest of the day? What would be your feelings about this issue?

　　•

　　•

3. When you return home, what would you tell your family about the incident? How do you think they would react?

　　•

　　•

4. Are there any special strategies which you think you would use to help yourself through the following days and weeks?

　　•

　　•

DISCUSSION OF EXERCISE 4:3

 ***1. Who would you want to speak to within the first HOUR following the attack?***

As you thought about this question, did you think of particular people that you would seek out, and any people whom you would try to avoid?

What were your thoughts about contacting people in authority or with special responsibility for your safety at work e.g. your line manager, the personnel officer? Were all of the people you thought of colleagues, or did you think about contacting friends or your partner, for example?

> *"In times of stress it is clearly a good thing to seek out the support of those whom you think we can trust to be helpful."*

In times of stress it is clearly a good thing to seek out the support of those whom we think we can trust to be helpful. They may help by listening, and by offering emotional support, advice, and practical help. However, you may have borne in mind the fact that not all colleagues and acquaintances are equally supportive, friendly, trustworthy, or charitable. Some people are natural healers who always seem to be pleasant and helpful, but on the other and some people seem naturally to take pleasure in magnifying problems and winding people up. Obviously these are best avoided, particularly during an acutely stressful period.

When some people are under emotional pressure they tend to dive for cover and prefer not to talk about the situation to anyone. They prefer to keep things to themselves and not to burden anyone else with their feelings and problems. Such people might be labelled 'silent sufferers'. At the other extreme, there are people, 'the trouble transmitters', who try to tell their story to as many people as possible. When you were answering the first question of the exercise, did you have difficulty in thinking of *anybody* you would wish to confide in, or did you immediately come up with a long list? In other words, does your answer to the question suggest that you tend towards being a 'silent sufferer' or a 'trouble transmitter'? By the way, there is no preferred answer to this question - no single strategy works best for everybody. But it is good to think in advance what would work best for you.

If ever the worst does happen - and we hope it won't - remember you can refer back to this!

2. *Would you wish to keep working for the rest of the day? What would be your feelings about this issue?*

Again, people differ widely in their response to this question. Some insist on carrying on as normal even after a truly grim episode. Others leave the workplace immediately, and request a period of leave for a week or so after their emotionally bruising episode.

Judging by your answer to Question 2, are you a more of a stayer or do you tend towards the escape end of the spectrum?

Again, it's very difficult to say what strategy is best. A person wanting to carry on despite everything may signify their determination not to let the episode get to them, or they may simply be one of those few people who are emotionally unscathed by an aggressive incident. Arranging to take some time off may allow a person to get over the attack and to start afresh the next day or the next week. Opting to have some time off could therefore be a healthy decision, indicating that the person is determined to look after him/herself. Those who encourage a person in this position to take some leave may be indicating their recognition that what happened deserves to be taken seriously.

However, insistence on carrying on as normal might suggest that the person is engaging in a form of psychological denial, and it is possible that there *may* be a price to pay for this in the longer-term. Similarly, staying away from work for a lengthy period after an attack may be unwise. One reason for this is that it may lead to an effect labelled the 'incubation of fear', i.e. if a person is absent from a situation or setting in which a traumatic event has occurred, they may develop a kind of phobia about the situation. If the last experience of the workplace was that of a traumatic attack, the thought of returning to the situation again may be very frightening, and the longer the person avoids returning to the situation the more the fear may develop.

Hence the colloquial piece of advice to get straight back on the horse we have just fallen off.

We were recently asked to run a post-incident workshop for a probation team that had experienced a serious violent incident in which a client had effectively held up the entire probation office. Three personnel ended up in the casualty department of the local hospital and several others, officers and office staff, were left in a state of severe shock. The attack had taken place in the summer, on a Friday, and two of the people involved went on their planned summer holiday immediately following the incident. Although they were not among the injured, these two people, who were absent from the office for the two weeks after the attack, seemed to have been the most severely affected by the incident in the longer term. When we ran our workshop, several months after the incident, one of these had not returned to work and the other was receiving psychiatric treatment for stress and depression. The one case doesn't prove anything, of course, but it does suggest that, rather than helping recovery, the two weeks holiday may have actually exacerbated the problem.

On balance, a fairly prompt return to work would seem to be the best recommendation. However, this should not be taken to extremes. Indeed, a very common response is for the person to insist that they will be alright and that 'the show MUST go on'. In the probation case cited above the three personnel returned to their jobs directly from casualty and continued to see clients throughout the afternoon. A balance must be struck between two potentially dangerous extremes, that of bolting away from the traumatic situation, in some cases never to return, and that of sticking to one's post when in dire need of a break, a rest, and a change of scene. Sometimes the victim is not in the best position to make a decision, and they may need friendly help and persuasion, as well as permission, from colleagues and managers.

Let's turn to the next question:

3. When you return home, what would you tell your family about the incident? How do you think they would react?

People differ very significantly in their responses to this question. Some can't wait to tell their partner, for example, and look forward to the support that they know they will get. Others feel that family members might be less than sympathetic, perhaps engaging in victim blaming, and some people say that they would avoid the issue at home in case the family were alarmed and became fearful whenever they went off to work.

Answering this question may have set you thinking about the degree to which we maintain a boundary between our home life and our life at work. Some people try to integrate the two as far as possible, while others do whatever they can to keep them separate.

And lastly,

4. Are there any special strategies which you think you would use to help yourself through the following days and weeks?

Some people say that they would wish to go through the incident in their minds and try to learn from their experience. Others say that they would try to take things easy for a while. Some report that they would seek out sympathetic people to talk to, and a few mention seeking professional help in the form of counselling. Some say that they would give themselves a special treat as a form of compensation for what they have been through. And others, of course, insist that they would just try to forget the whole thing as soon as possible.

Before we leave the topic of self-help following an incident, let's note a few other points:

- We should recognize that some degree of self-blame is natural, but try not to be too self-critical.

- If we *do* feel that our behaviour during the incident was less than perfect, we should remind ourselves that everybody makes mistakes – this does NOT imply that we are unfit for the job. We try to master the skill of taking the relevant learning points without heaping blame upon yourself!

- Be prepared for some tension at a de-briefing stage - e.g. a manager may need to assess whether we were at fault.

- We should take time before considering such long-term issues as a possible change of role or specialism, and our future contact with the aggressive person.

- *In due course,* consider what might be learned from the incident.

  - What might YOU learn?

  - What might your COLLEAGUES learn?

  - What might your AGENCY learn?

We turn now to a consideration of what we might do if one of our colleagues had been attacked.

CHAPTER 4:2.2

HELPING A COLLEAGUE WHO HAS BEEN ATTACKED

There are many things that we can do to help a colleague who has been attacked, both IN THE SHORTER TERM (i.e. immediately after the incident), and IN THE LONGER TERM ...

1) IN THE SHORTER TERM

1. Give any First Aid that might be necessary, or see that medical help is obtained.

First the matter of **First Aid:**

- Have you yourself been trained in first aid?   YES / NO

- Is first aid training available (for you) within your agency?
                                        YES / NO / DON'T KNOW

- Is there an appointed first-aider within your work area?
                                        YES / NO / DON'T KNOW

- If there is, who is it? ....

Becoming trained in first aid yourself, and knowing the name of your designated first-aider, are examples of precautions. They are very useful precautions for all kinds of accidents as well as an emergency following an attack.

A second point concerning first aid or medical help concerns the attitude of the person who has been attacked. Very often they will not want to make a fuss and will deny that their injuries require medical attention. We might not agree, and this can give rise to a delicate situation. We might try various kinds of persuasion, including the line: *"Just let them look you over, at least then I'd be a little happier"*, but beware of being too conscientious and insisting that they MUST receive attention.

A set of dilemmas: The question of how much to make of an attack is delicate, and it applies not only to the question of arranging for the person to receive medical attention but also to a number of other issues.

With someone trying to play down the attack made upon them, we may find that we are in dispute over such matters as: making a report; informing a manager;

making a formal complaint against the aggressor; calling the police; leaving the workplace; alerting relatives; taking time off; and seeking professional psychological or counselling help. In all of these cases a balance needs to be drawn between over-playing the situation and under-playing it.

> "Any hostile action or threat
> SHOULD be noted – so that it can at least
> be put on record as a warning to others
> who may later come
> into contact with the aggressor."

There are no hard and fast rules, but at least we should be aware that our judgement may differ from the victim's, with the victim trying to play down the incident. There is clearly a limit to how much we should insist, in the victim's best interest, on the course of action that we feel to be wise. Sometimes the matter is best left to a manager who has the legitimate power to insist on a particular course of action, the power to grant leave, etc. We should, however, be firm on the matter of reporting any serious aggressive incident. Any hostile action or threat SHOULD be noted - so that it can at least be put on record as a warning to others who may later come into contact with the aggressor.

2. Offer to lift the victim's immediate burden of work

Offering to inform the appropriate manager about the incident, and to take over urgent work tasks, are all important ways in which a colleague may lighten their immediate burden of work.

3. Give emotional support

We can do this by providing reassurance and giving our colleague time and space to talk about the assault. However - another dilemma - don't insist that s/he *must* talk about the attack - recognize that some people prefer not to talk about such things. That is their right, although at some later point they may have to give their account of the incident to a manager, or in a de-briefing session or, more rarely, to the police.

4. Offer to take the victim home

If it has been agreed that the best course of action is for the colleague to leave the workplace, consider travelling home with him/her. If we do this, we might also offer to stay until a friend or a relative arrives. If the attack has been fairly serious it would be unwise to leave the victim alone. We can also offer to contact the person's partner, or a relative or friend. It might be useful to stay for just a little while after the other person has arrived, to help set the scene before we hand over.

The above description implies that we are the main helper among the group of colleagues. If our role is more peripheral, for example because someone else has taken the main support role, then we can still help by taking care not to avoid the victim, by not making light of the situation, by offering sympathy, and by volunteering but not insisting upon, a listening ear and practical help.

2) IN THE LONGER TERM

Our support for the victim should not be confined to the immediate aftermath of an attack. Some colleagues are very helpful in the short term, but their interest and concern for the victim soon fade. In many cases special support is necessary for some days or weeks until the victim makes a good adjustment. If s/he has taken time off work, then the process of getting back to the job, facing colleagues, and re-integrating with the team, may be difficult and painful. In some cases the most severe psychological effects become apparent only some time after the assault. We can help by continuing to give personal support, by communicating with others in our team, (although this should not amount to gossiping) and by relaying any positive and supportive messages from colleagues and managers.

> *"A listening ear and practical help"*

We should keep an eye on our colleague without being invasive or overbearing. Be sensitive to any indication that the person has begun to find our attention and concern somewhat irritating, and try not to be over-sensitive about this - it may be part of an adjustment process, the colleague's way of saying: *"I'm alright now, I'm getting over things in my own way"*. Sometimes the victim will look back upon the time, immediately after the attack, when they felt helpless and were highly dependent on us. They may now be embarrassed about this, and in their reassertion of independence they may even show a slight resentment of their former dependency. Again, this is something that can be hurtful. It is less likely to offend us, however, if we understand and anticipate that such a response is a possible stage in the victim's attempt to get back to normal.

LESSENING THE EFFECTS OF AN INCIDENT
helping a friend or colleague: summary

<u>In the short-term we can:</u>

- Give any first aid, or see that medical help is obtained.

- Offer to take over urgent work tasks

- Contact colleague's line manager to report the incident

- Provide reassurance and sympathy

- Give colleague time and 'space' to talk about the assault (but recognize that some prefer not to talk about it)

- Consider travelling home with the colleague (and then waiting until a relative arrives)

- Contact relatives or neighbours

<u>In the longer-term, we can:</u>

- Continue to offer support

- Be available to talk about developments such as:

  - other colleagues' reactions

  - legal consequences of the assault

  - professional consequences

- Support colleague in deriving lessons from the assault and proposing any changes in procedures or environment.

EXERCISE 4:4

Which of the measures summarised above do you judge to
be most important?

Why?

CHAPTER 4:2.3

THE MANAGER'S ROLE

It is clearly important that managers should know about their duties and responsibilities following an attack, and about the useful things they may do to help the victim (both the DO's and the DON'Ts). But it is also important that victims themselves and their colleagues understand the role and responsibilities of the manager in such circumstances. The aim of this section is to consider some of the relevant issues. We begin with an exercise - an exercise in which you role-play (on paper at least) being a manager.

EXERCISE 4:5

THE MANAGER'S ROLE FOLLOWING AN ATTACK

Put yourself in the role of the line-manager of someone who has been attacked. What are your DUTIES and TASKS

a) to the victim

b) to your organisation?

Think about what you would need to do both IMMEDIATELY and in the LONGER TERM.

List as many immediate and longer term duties and tasks as you can think of in your role as manager, in the spaces provided overleaf.

1) DUTIES TOWARDS THE VICTIM - SHORTER TERM

-
-
-
-
-

2) DUTIES TOWARDS THE VICTIM - LONGER TERM

-
-
-
-
-

3) DUTIES TOWARDS YOUR ORGANISATION - SHORTER TERM

-
-
-
-
-

4) DUTIES TOWARDS YOUR ORGANISATION - LONGER TERM

-
-
-
-

DISCUSSION OF EXERCISE 4:5

1) DUTIES TOWARDS THE VICTIM - SHORTER TERM

Assuming that you have been informed of an attack immediately after it has occurred, the following things may need to be done URGENTLY:

- Ensure that the aggressor is no longer a danger to colleagues, or to others, or to 'the public'.

- Think about whether you need to contact the police (a) to call for help or (b) to report the incident. (If you <u>are</u> the police, this doesn't apply as much!)

- Ensure that the victim is being given any necessary medical attention. You may need to arrange first aid or hospital treatment.

- Ensure that the person is being looked after by a colleague.

- Speak with the victim to assure him/her of your managerial support and to ascertain his/her immediate needs and wishes.

- Decide whether the victim needs to take time off work, balancing the need for recovery time with the possible adverse effects that may stem from an 'incubation of fear'.

- Consider whether you need to temporarily restructure workloads, etc. in order to lighten the immediate burden of work for the victim, and decide how you will do this.

2) DUTIES TOWARDS THE VICTIM - LONGER TERM

In the hours and days that follow the attack, keep in touch with the victim, preferably by meeting with them but otherwise by telephone. *Many victims of serious attacks report that a visit to their home by a manager left a lasting impression of support.*

Such a visit seems to be regarded as a sign that there is real concern for them as a person as well as a worker. It can also provide an assurance that the manager and the service are taking the matter very seriously.

Such meetings or telephone conversations have a number of important functions:

- *They help us to remain in touch with the victim's feelings, wishes, and plans (which may change considerably from day to day)*

- *They help us to keep the victim in touch with developments relating to the attack, both at team level and at management level*

- *They may help to prevent the victim feeling 'abandoned' by colleagues and the organisation (such feelings might make a return to work extremely difficult).*

During conversations with the victim, it may be necessary to establish:

- *The victim's attitude to working again under the same conditions*

- *The victim's feelings about a possible de-briefing meeting with colleagues*

- *The victim's plans, if any, for starting legal proceedings against the attacker*

- *The victim's need for help on legal and insurance matters*

- *The extent to which the victim feels a need for professional counselling.*

3) DUTIES TO THE ORGANISATION - SHORTER TERM

As well as the duties and tasks needed to help the victim directly, there are many things that may need to be done in the interest of the organisation. These include:

- Establishing the nature of the attack, together with

what led up to it, including the actions taken by the victim throughout the incident. The victim, and possibly colleagues, will therefore need to be thoroughly de-briefed.

> *"We should consider the agency's and the victim's future roles with respect to the aggressor."*

Notes should be taken at the time, and a copy of the report sent to the appropriate authorities, with a copy to the victim. The victim may be asked to check the report for accuracy, and may submit a note indicating their agreement, or any points of disagreement, with the account.

If possible, eg. in residential settings, it may be necessary to obtain an account of the incident from the aggressor.

- The issue of whether permanent or semi-permanent changes need to be made in the nature of the victim's work may require consideration. Any such changes should be discussed with the victim, who should not be made to feel - if any such changes are implemented - that this indicates a critical or blaming attitude on the part of management. Ultimately, of course, any such re-allocation of duties must remain the prerogative of the manager, in the best interest of the service, its employees and its clients.

4) DUTIES TO THE ORGANISATION - LONGER TERM

We should consider holding a special meeting for all staff who were involved in the incident, and perhaps other colleagues as well, to provide for a general de-briefing and to allow for the open airing of feelings and different points of view.

Ideally the victim would be present at such a meeting, but in some cases they may be unable to face a detailed reconstruction of the incident. In any case the situation is likely to be delicate and should be handled with the utmost tact and care.

Remember that some colleagues might wish to attribute a substantial part of the blame to the victim, and we should plan what we will do if this occurs

De-briefing meetings are often highly constructive, allowing lessons to be learned from the incident, prompting suggestions for further precautionary measures, and signalling solidarity and emotional support for the victim. At their best they can be highly productive and therapeutic. However, it has to be recognized that such meetings can also be fraught, confrontational, and destructive. When they go wrong, they may lead to people taking sides, and they may sap the morale of colleagues, managers and, especially, the victim. There are often many important lessons to be learned from an aggressive incident.

Our interview with the victim, and the information we glean from the de-briefing meeting and from interactions with the victim's colleagues, might well suggest that certain procedures need revision, or that further resources are needed; the provision of personal alarms, for example. We should implement any changes as swiftly as possible and pass information and recommendations to relevant personnel throughout the agency.

We should consider the agency's and the victim's future roles with respect to the aggressor. We may feel that there should be no future contact between the victim and the attacker, and, depending on the organisation, we may wish to recommend that the organisation discontinue its offer of services to the person in question, if statutory duties permit. In making any such a recommendation it is important to take account of the victim's own views.

In some cases we may also have an opportunity and a duty to interview the aggressor. One function of such an interview will be to hear his or her own version of the incident. It is of course necessary to stress the unacceptability and indefensibility of the attack. At the same interview, or at a later date, we should also spell out the consequences of the incident for the attacker. This may include information about whether legal action is to be taken and - for some organisations - whether or not the organisation is prepared to continue providing a service to the person, and under what conditions. *As a manager, we may have a major role to play in considering whether the agency should begin legal proceedings. This calls for wide consultation with all concerned.*

Finally, we should ensure that information relating to the assault is recorded centrally, and that the matter is brought to the attention of relevant agency officials.

The Manager's Role - A General Note

It will be recognized from the above discussion that the manager has many different roles to play following a serious aggressive incident. S/he has to act as counsellor, investigator, human resources manager, information co-ordinator, policy-maker, etc. Some of these roles make conflicting demands, and all call for tact, diplomacy and sensitivity!

LESSENING THE EFFECTS OF AN INCIDENT
a summary of the manager's role

The manager has a very extensive list of tasks, some of which seem to be in conflict with each other. He or she should endeavour to:

- Arrange hospital treatment if necessary.

- Ensure that aggressor is no longer a danger.

- Contact police if necessary.

- Ensure that victim is being appropriately looked after.

- De-brief the victim. Make notes.

- Consider whether time off is needed (but bear in mind the 'incubation of fear' phenomenon).

- Re-allocate victim's workload.

- Obtain full information on the incident from all of those present (including, if possible, the aggressor) and ensure that details are fully recorded.

- Consider holding a special meeting for all staff involved, to provide a general de-briefing and an open airing of feelings.

- Derive learning points and consider changes in procedures and resources .

- Implement changes as swiftly as possible and disseminate information throughout the agency.

- Consider what the agency's and victim's role with respect to the aggressor will be in the future.

- In certain settings, the manager may have the opportunity and the duty to interview the aggressor and make plain the unacceptability of what s/he has done.

- Consider whether agency / victim/ police might wish to start legal proceedings.

- Consult all of those involved in this decision.

- Consider whether the victim needs professional counselling.

- Ensure that information relating to the assault is recorded centrally, so that it is incorporated into a central monitoring procedure.

- Recognize that the role of manager following a serious incident is a difficult one, calling on many different roles - counsellor, investigator, human resources manager, etc.

CHAPTER 4:3

CONCLUSION

This Module has dealt with two major topics:

- *The psychological after-effects of an attack*

- *What can be done by the victim, colleagues, and managers to reduce such after-effects*

We have also suggested that careful consideration of an attack or threat may lead to important lessons being learned by the victim, by colleagues and by the organisation as a whole. It is a sad truth that certain precautions may be implemented only *after* an attack.

INFORMATION - RESOLUTION - ACTION

One of the purposes of this course has been to help you to suggest and implement precautions *before* an attack occurs. Hopefully the course has led you to consider carefully the physical aspects of your work setting, the preparations you might make with your colleagues for action in an emergency, and many aspects of your work. It is certainly our expectation that this course will have sensitized you to certain changes which need to be made to increase your safety.

But sensitization is only part of the solution - the key is ACTION.

It may not be New Year's Day, but this is a day on which you might consider making some resolutions.

PAUSE FOR THOUGHT

Think over the course content. Look back at particular parts of the course if you need to and write down some resolutions about how you intend to change things in order to make your working life SAFER.

If you have already implemented changes as a result of participating in this course, then you may also wish to include these on your list. Here are some prompts to help ...

PROMPTS:

- *What new personal precautions will you be taking?*

- *How will you change your physical working environment?*

- *Are there suggestions / recommendations which you would wish to make to your manager, or to write to your Safety Committee about?*

- *Are there particular aspects of your working practice that you wish to discuss with your colleagues? For example, will you be arranging a telephone emergency message?*

- *How do you intend to change your practice, for example with regard to scheduling, home visits, or making yourself even more approachable and available?*

These are just a few suggestions - the material included in the course could help to make literally hundreds of resolutions. List your most important resolutions in the spaces below:

1. ....

2. ....

3. ....

4. ....

5. ....

COURSE CONCLUSION

We hope that you have found the course interesting, and that you will implement at least some of the suggestions in order to reduce the risks you may face in the course of your work.

You may wish to revise certain parts of the course in order to feel confident about dealing with threatening situations in the future.

It would hardly be surprising if at this stage you can remember very little of the material you have been reading. However, your task was not to learn information by heart. The reading you have done, and your active participation in the various exercises, will have changed your thinking more than you probably realize. If a threatening incident should

occur in the future you will be better prepared to handle it, not because you will remember word-for-word what you have read in this learning programme, but your active participation means that you will have rehearsed many different ways of dealing with difficult situations. Having rehearsed strategies mentally, we are more likely to use them if the need should arise.

As we said at the beginning of Module One, going through a programme such as this will not guarantee that we will never be attacked. But it should have significantly reduced the risk that we will be injured, especially if we manage to change our working environment along the lines suggested in the sections on Precautions.

And if we are ever unfortunate enough to be attacked, our knowledge about the

possible psychological consequences of an attack may well serve to reduce the after-effects. Knowing in advance that some colleagues may be awkward, evasive, and less than 100% supportive following an attack may make such responses easier to tolerate. And if a colleague is attacked then we will be better prepared to respond in a helpful way.

SOME FINAL THOUGHTS:

Take Personal Responsibility For Your Own Safety

Be Mindful Of Potential Dangers And Take Adequate Precautions. And Remember That Your Employers Also Have Responsibilities Regarding Your Safety.

> *"Remember, our safety is a shared responsibility,*
> *partly it is our employer's,*
> *but it is also ours."*

Don't Feel That You Have To Be Brave

Recognize the limits to your capacity for dealing with difficult situations and don't go unprotected into situations that you believe to be highly dangerous. Don't be afraid to ask for help when you need it. Be assertive in the cause of your own safety. If you need to see someone in their home, and you are dreading the visit, ask for someone to accompany you. If you have an appointment to see someone whom you believe to be dangerous, ask for someone to join you in the meeting.

Work Towards Changing Any Dangerous Attitudes That You Still Hold

Could you be accused of holding any of the following attitudes?
"I must be able to deal with anything and anybody"
"I must never show that I am afraid"
"Even in extreme danger I must not lose face or run away"
If so, work towards changing them. 'Must' statements allow for no exceptions, and they are therefore unrealistic and can be dangerous.

Beware Of Your Own Aggression

We should not forget that some professionals have been known to become violent towards clients. If we find ourselves becoming angry, we need to work on our appraisals and call upon our inhibitions. The costs involved if *we* become aggressive are too obvious to need repeating.

Back Your Own Judgement

Occasionally we just know in our hearts that a particular action would be just the wrong thing to do. Pay heed to those feelings, it's surprising how often they are right!

... AND ABSOLUTELY FINALLY

Having completed this course you will have spent between eight and ten hours concentrating on one relatively small part of your professional role - the danger zone.

Training in this area is, however, increasingly recognized as an important part of post-qualification experience. Employers are more aware than ever before of the need to provide relevant training opportunities for their employees, and every time there is another newspaper report of a professional being attacked and seriously injured the pressure for such training increases.

BUT let us keep things in perspective. There is a danger that a course such as this can over-sensitize us to the risks we might face in our work. We have been considering only the 'downside'. We should not forget that working with most people is both safe and rewarding. Thankfully, most people rarely encounter seriously dangerous situations, and as the Crimewatch television presenter reminds us at the end of every programme: *"such things are relatively rare; please don't lose too much sleep"*.

Why, then, so much effort to understand aggression and to protect professionals? The answer is that when aggression *does* occur its consequences can be severe, especially if things are handled badly. And the other reason is that many of the strategies that are useful in dealing with aggression and hostility have a much wider relevance. They can help us to reduce the stress that may come from working with particular people and may help us to further develop our skill in coming across as helpful, approachable and caring.

Rowett, C. (1986) Violence in Social Work. *Institute of Criminology Occasional Papers, No. 14.* Cambridge University.

Wexler, D.B. (2000) *Domestic Violence 2000.* W W Norton.

FORENSIC SERVICES AND THE PRISON SERVICE

Davies, W. (1982) Violence in Prisons. In M.P.Feldman (Ed.) *Developments in the Study of Criminal Behaviour, Volume 2, Violence,* Chichester: Wiley.

Davies, W. (1997) *A Cognitive Approach to Working with Offenders.* The APT Press, Leicester.

Davies, W. and Burgess, P.W. (1988) Prison Officers' Experience as a Predictor of Risk of Attack: An Analysis Within the British Prison System. *Medicine, Science and the Law,* 28, 135-8.

Davies, W. and Burgess, P.W. (1988) The Effect of Management Regime on Disruptive Behaviour: An Analysis within the British Prison System. *Medicine, Science and The Law,* 28, 243-7.

Kinzel, A.F. (1970) Body-Buffer Zones in Violent Prisoners. *American Journal of Psychiatry,* 127, 59-64.

Novaco, R. (1985) Anger and its Therapeutic Regulation. In M.A.Chesney and R.H.Roseman (Eds.) *Anger and Hostility in Cardiovascular and Behavioural Disorders.* New York: Hemisphere Publishing Corporation.

CHILDREN AND ADOLESCENTS / COMMUNITY HOMES /SCHOOLS

Cameron, R., Bailey, M. and Wallis, J. (1984) Difficult and Disruptive Behaviour: I. Reconciling Needs of Clients and Staff. *Mental Handicap, 12,* 45-97.

Feindler, E.L. and Ecton, R.B. (1986) *Adolescent Anger Control: Cognitive Behavioural Techniques.* Oxford: Pergamon.

Frude, N. (1989) Physical Child Abuse. In: K. Hollin and K. Howells (Eds.) *Clinical Approaches to Violence.* Chichester: Wiley.

Gentry, M.R. and Ostapiuk, E.B. (1989) Violence in institutions for young offenders and disturbed adolescents. In: K. Howells and C.R. Hollin (Eds.) *Clinical Approaches to Violence.* Chichester: Wiley.

Lamplugh, D. & Pagan, B. (1996) *Personal Safety for Schools.* Arena.

Millham, S., Bullock, R. and Hosie, K. (1976) On Violence in Community Homes. In: N. Tutt (Ed.) *Violence*. London: HMSO.

FURTHER READING

GENERAL – AGGRESSION and EXTREME BEHAVIOUR

Argyle, M. (1988) *Bodily Communication,* 2nd Edition. London: Methuen.

Davies, W. (1988) How Not to Get Hit. *The Psychologist,* May 1988.

Davies, W. (2000) *Overcoming Anger and Irritability*. Robinson.

Davies, W. (2000) *Overcoming Anger and Irritability: A Clinician's Guide.* The APT Press, Leicester.

Davies, W. (2000) *The RAID® Manual.* The APT Press, Leicester.

Eysenck, H.J. (1968) A Theory of the Incubation of Anxiety/Fear Responses. *Behaviour Research and Therapy*, 6, 309-21.

Haley, R. (2000) *Fear of Violence*. Robert Hale.

Mason, T. and Chandley, M. (1999) *Management of Violence and Aggression.* Churchill Livingstone.

Mayhew, P., Maung, A.E. and Mirrlees-Black, C. (1993) *The 1992 British Crime Survey.* London: Her Majesty's Stationery Office.

GENERAL - VIOLENCE IN THE WORKPLACE

Anon (1994) *Violence at Work: a Guide for Employers, Pack.* London: The Health and Safety Executive.

Anon (1995) *Preventing Violence to Retail Staff.* London: The Health and Safety Executive.

Braverman, M. (1999) *Preventing Workplace Violence.* Sage USA

Chappell, D. and Di Martino, V. (2000) *Violence at Work.* The Brookings Institution.

Davies, W. (1989) The Prevention of Assault on Professional Helpers. In: K. Hollin and K. Howells (Eds.) *Clinical Approaches to Violence.* Chichester: Wiley.

Ishmael, A. *Harassment, Bullying and Violence at Work.* London: The Industrial Society.

Kinney, J.A. (1995) *Violence at Work.*

Leather, P. et al (eds) (1998) *Work Related Violence.* Routledge.

Trewartha, R, and Leadbetter, D. (1995) *Handling Aggression and Violence at Work.* Russell HousePublishing

Turnbull, J. & Patterson, B. (1999) *Aggression and Violence.* Palgrove.

Wilkinson, C.W. (ed.) (1998) *Violence in the Workplace: Preventing, Assessing and Managing of Threats at Work.*

HEALTH SERVICES

Davies, W., Katz, J. and Anstiss, D. (1988) Token Changes. *Nursing Times,* December 1988.

DHSS (1989) Report of the DHSS Advisory Committee on Violence to Staff (Violence to Staff). London, HMSO.

Miller, R. (1990) *Managing Difficult Patients: A Guide for Nurses and Other Health Workers.* London: Faber and Faber.

Royal College of Nursing and Royal College of Psychiatrists (1986) Principles of Good Medical and Nursing Practice in the Management of Acts of Violence. London: RCN and RCP.

Royal College of Nursing (1987) Guidelines for Dealing with Aggression in the Accident and Emergency Department. London, RCN.

Wykes, T. (ed.) (1994) *Violence and Health Care Professionals.* Nelson Thornes.

SOCIAL SERVICES

Brady, E. (1993) *Coping with Violent Behaviour. A Handbook for Social Work Staff.* London: Longman.

Browne, K. and Herbert, M. (1996) *Preventing Family Violence.* Wiley and Sons.

Donnellan, C. (1999) *Dealing with Domestic Violence.* Independence Educational Publishers.

Norris, D. & Kedward, C. (1990) *Violence Against Social Workers: The Implications for Practice.* London: Jessica Kingsley.

NOTES

NOTES